GERARD MANLEY HOPKINS

THE MAN AND THE POET

by
K. R. SRINIVASA IYENGAR

With a Foreword by
JEROME D'SOUZA, S.J.

INDIAN BRANCH
GEOFFREY CUMBERLEGE
OXFORD UNIVERSITY PRESS

Oxford University Press, Amen House, London E.C. 4
EDINBURGH GLASGOW NEW YORK TORONTO MELBOURNE
WELLINGTON BOMBAY CALCUTTA MADRAS CAPE TOWN
Geoffrey Cumberlege, Publisher to the University

First Published 1948

PRINTED IN INDIA
By P. C. Ray at Sri Gouranga Press, 5, Chintamani Das Lane, Calcutta, and published by Geoffrey Cumberlege, Oxford University Press, Calcutta.

TO
V. K. AYAPPAN PILLAI

ALSO BY K. R. SRINIVASA IYENGAR

Sri Aurobindo
Lytton Strachey, A Critical Study
Indo-Anglian Literature
Literature & Authorship in India
Indian Contribution to English Literature
On Beauty
S. Srinivasa Iyengar
Raja Lakhamagauda
Musings of Basava (in collaboration)
A Handbook of Indian Administration
       (in collaboration)

EDITED BY K. R. SRINIVASA IYENGAR

Dryden's *Absalom & Achitophel*
Coleridge's *Christabel*
Congreve's *The Way of the World*
Indian Writers in Council

CONTENTS

		PAGE
	PREFACE	ix
	FOREWORD	xi
I.	INTRODUCTION	1
II.	BOYHOOD: EARLY POEMS	5
III.	OXFORD	14
IV.	CONVERSION	23
V.	OXFORD POETRY	30
VI.	THE LURE OF LOYOLA	41
VII.	PROBATION	51
VIII.	'THE WRECK OF THE *Deutschland*'	59
IX.	A ROLLING STONE	72
X.	HOPKINS AND DUNS SCOTUS	81
XI.	POEMS ON MAN AND NATURE	89
XII.	HOPKINS AND BRIDGES	100
XIII.	BAILLIE, DIXON AND PATMORE	111
XIV.	HOPKINS'S POLITICAL VIEWS	125
XV.	IRELAND: THE TERRIBLE SONNETS: LAST DAYS	132
XVI.	HOPKINS'S PROSODY	150
XVII.	TECHNICAL AND LINGUISTIC EXPERIMENTS	172
XVIII.	CONCLUSION	184
	SELECT BIBLIOGRAPHY	193

PREFACE

THIS book has grown out of three articles which I contributed to the *New Review* of Calcutta in 1938. The typescript was ready for the press as early as April 1939, but the actual publication of the book has had to be delayed so long on account of the war. Taking up the typescript after the lapse of nearly nine years, I have nevertheless resisted the temptation to make too many or too drastic changes in the original draft; I have, however, not failed to take advantage of fresh material on the subject published in the interval, to make some important qualifications in the text and add a few footnotes.

It is, perhaps, a foolhardy enterprise for an Indian and a Hindu to attempt a study of an English poet and a Jesuit priest. I took my B.A. degree in 1927 and M.A. degree (in English Language and Literature) some years later without so much as having heard of Hopkins. Mr R. L. Megroz's references to Hopkins in his *Modern English Poetry* (1933) first stimulated my interest in the poet no less than the Jesuit. The Rev. Jerome D'Souza, S.J., my old professor at St Xavier's, Palamcottah, now Principal of Loyola College, Madras, watched my enthusiasm for Hopkins with tender solicitude and helped me at every stage of my work. He arranged for the publication of my articles in the *New Review*; he replied to my queries in detail and he offered many a fruitful suggestion towards the improvement of my book; and, above all, he readily acceded to my request for a Foreword to this study of Hopkins the man and the poet. It is over twenty years since I listened as an undergraduate to the Rev. Jerome D'Souza's inspiring class lectures, and every year, every month, but increases my indebtedness to him.

I am also deeply indebted to the Oxford University Press for facilitating the publication of this book; to the University of Bombay for making a grant-in-aid towards the cost of publication; to the Editor of the *New Review* for permitting me to incorporate into the book the articles contributed to that paper; to Dr S. C. Nandimath, Principal, Basaveshvar College, Bagalkot, and Professor C. D. Pinto, St Xavier's, Bombay, for their sympathetic interest; and to Dr C. R. Reddy, Vice-Chancellor of the Andhra University, for his generous understanding and encouragement of my literary work during the seven years I have been privileged to know him.

K. R. SRINIVASA IYENGAR

Andhra University
Waltair
21 February 1948

FOREWORD

THE casual reader, English or Indian, taking up this book, is likely to be surprised that the personality and poetry of Gerard Manley Hopkins should have attracted the pen of an Indian scholar. Even now, Hopkins is not very widely known in England; and in India his name is familiar only to the very limited circle whose profession keeps them in touch with the movement of English Letters. And most of these, brought up on literary judgements based on Victorian standards, admirers of the verse of Tennyson, Swinburne and the earlier Yeats, were sure to be repelled by the 'oddities' of Hopkins's language and versification.

The content of Hopkins's poetry would be an even more effective barrier to a sympathetic encounter between him and the Indian critic. Hopkins's poetic effort is dominated by his religious convictions. Even where the primary impulse is natural, as in all the poems inspired by earthly beauty, the final expression represents a fusion of the natural experience with the realities and exigencies of the spiritual world. By his conversion to Catholicism and his life as a Religious of the Society of Jesus, these realities had entered and taken possession of his soul when it had been reduced to solitude by reflection, prayer, and the sacrifice of earthly ties. By a quality of his mind which we can only describe as 'intensity'—by which we mean an immense seriousness and thoroughness in all his activities —and by a total adhesion to the spirit of the Exercises of St Ignatius, these same spiritual realities, their tremendous import, the absolute nature of the claims they make on us, became the central facts in Gerard Hopkins's life, waking and sleeping. He had also a fierce intellectual passion for order, consistency, and unity. A divided house meant death for him. Thenceforth the drama of his inner life may be described as an effort to conquer, to transform, to integrate somehow, the activity of the senses with his spiritual outlook. The keenness of his sensibility, the passionate energy of his perceptions, his sense of colour and sound and form, his eye for the strangest and most astonishing resemblances, made this task of spiritual conquest a long and agonizing one. His poetic work is a faithful reflection of the changing fortunes of that struggle. At times it seemed to him that the only solution was the suppression of the activity of the senses and the stifling of the poet in him. At others, his inability to suppress it and his failure to divinize it caused those moods of dejection of which the 'terrible' sonnets are the enduring expression. There is no doubt that this process of purification, so bitter and so sweet, left a permanent mark on his character and health. No wonder he acted oddly at times; no wonder he seemed something of a 'character' to fellow Jesuits who—even they—little suspected the nature of his interior life; that the struggle left him exhausted and led to a premature death. But it is certain that before the end he had resolved the moral tension and attained peace. Surely the 'Spiritual Exercises' themselves, whose virtue it is to wound in order to heal, to kill in order to revivify, gave him the secret of that peace. For in the 'Contemplation to obtain Love', does not the austere Ignatius, poet, humanist, and ascetic all in one, does not Ignatius teach his children to recognize the beauty of the world as descending from above like rays from the sun and waters from the spring? Hopkins was further helped thereto by the Platonic element in Christian philosophy, an element perceptible in St Thomas himself, but pervasive in Patristic and in Franciscan tradition, in Duns Scotus whom he hailed as a kindred spirit, 'of realty the rarest-veined unraveller'. Whatever the process, after the days of his mourning, he turned his sometime averted gaze on a transformed world and saw it 'charged with the grandeur of God'. In almost every poem this new vision finds expression. Perhaps the 'Blessed Virgin compared to the Air we Breathe' is the happiest example of this fusion of nature and grace.

Now such a spiritual process will be intelligible only to a very few even among Christian readers. Bridges, great poet and devoted friend, failed to appreciate the import of Hopkins's 'Marianism' and asceticism. What likelihood was there that a non-Christian scholar would do justice to the deepest springs of this complex character? Nevertheless, the reader of the following pages will see that Dr Srinivasa Iyengar has overcome these obstacles and produced a study adequate to his subject from almost every point of view. The character of Hopkins is described and his life story narrated with deep understanding and every relevant detail. The problems of religious psychology are squarely faced and the fundamental place of the religious quest in Hopkins's development brought out with admirable fairness. The lights and shades of his temperament are clearly marked and very quickly the reader gets the impress of a remarkable personality, delicate and sensitive on the surface, but with great underlying strength and force of character, a warm humanity, and an overmastering force of perception, intellectual and imaginative.

Not less noteworthy is Dr Srinivasa Iyengar's treatment of the technique of Hopkins's verse. Here, more than in other branches of criticism, sureness and, especially, originality of judgement are difficult for a foreign student. The best that can be ordinarily done in this line by the Indian critic is a judicious assimilation of the opinions of English masters. I venture to think that the author has gone beyond this in his analysis of Hopkins's verse. He has not only understood the mechanism of it, but has realized the significance of its metrical innovations, taken keen delight in the new rhythms and assonances with which Hopkins has enriched English poetry. In a word this study is the fruit of a genuine though discriminating enthusiasm.

That is the secret of the strength and clarity of the finest of these pages, their warmth and precision, the force and penetration of their judgements.

I hope the author will forgive me if I venture to indicate here some reasons of a personal order which have enabled him to achieve such striking success in the appraisal of a Jesuit poet. The physiognomy of Jesuit priests is familiar to a large number of Indian intellectuals who, like Dr Srinivasa Iyengar, have passed through their many colleges in India. The knowledge of their training and outlook which Dr Iyengar gained in his college days has been completed by extensive reading of modern Catholic literature, of Chesterton and Belloc, of Etienne Gilson and Jacques Maritain, of Christopher Dawson, Edward Watkin and Alfred Noyes. There is no doubt that these special contacts have prevented that bias against Catholicism which every student of English Protestant literature is likely to receive, and given to Dr Iyengar an unusual insight into the religious life of Father Hopkins.

These are days of far-reaching changes in the educational system of India. The future of English studies in this country is uncertain. The English language will not long retain the privileged position it has hitherto had in the curricula of secondary and higher education. But the days of its primacy have not been barren of achievement. However, among the works of admitted excellence—poems, novels, history, biography and autobiography—which India has contributed to the storehouse of English Letters, literary criticism of English authors occupies necessarily the narrowest place. Dr Srinivasa Iyengar is in the front rank among the few who have gained distinction in this field. And those acquainted with his work will, I think, agree that this study of Hopkins is the finest piece of work he has yet done, and will wish it the diffusion and permanence to which the maturity and finish of its workmanship entitle it. His scholarship has recently received well merited recognition by his appointment as Professor of English Literature in the Andhra University. With the advantages which this position will afford him, he may be confidently expected to give us in the coming years studies of comparative, if not greater, excellence in the vast field of English Literature.

JEROME D'SOUZA, S.J.

Loyola College
Madras
17 February 1948

I. INTRODUCTION

WE often read learned discourses on 'modern' English poetry, 'modernist' poetry, 'recent' poetry, the 'new' poetry, and so on; and we idly listen to tyros in literary criticism talking of tendencies, movements, reactions, the *'Zeitgeist'*, trying to explain the poetry of today in terms of such intriguing abstractions. One seeks to evolve order out of the chaos of hundreds of poets essaying verse by grouping them all roughly into 'Right' and 'Left' poets, in other words into 'Traditionalists' and 'Innovators'. But here too a strange irony trips us into discomfiture. For, the extreme 'Left' poets who are talked about today—a Wystan Auden, a Cecil Day Lewis, a Stephen Spender, a Henry Treece—and who are younger than the T. S. Eliots, Ezra Pounds, and Herbert Reads of yesterday, and much younger than the Masefields, de la Mares, and Kiplings of the day before, are seemingly studious disciples, not so much of the poets of yesterday or the day before, but of the comparatively remote Gerard Manley Hopkins, chronologically almost a mid-Victorian poet! How convenient to summarize all twentieth-century poetry as a clear and conscious reaction against the complacent Victorianism of the great Tennyson and his smaller satellites. How very thrilling to be allowed to watch a poetic battle royal between the 'modernists' led by Eliot, Pound and Auden (not to mention the impossible Cummings) and the 'old guard', championed by a Sturge Moore, a Martin Armstrong, a Lascelles Abercrombie. How fascinating to trace the vicissitudes of 'modernism' through the 'experiments' and 'achievements' of the writers of *vers libres*, dadaists, islanders, imagists, polyphonists, vorticists, neo-impressionists, surrealists, futurists, and the other bewildering constellations on the twentieth-century poetic firmament. But, again and again, Hopkins all but upturns these neat apple carts of contemporary criticism.

Indeed, one who honestly reads poetry rather than gropes about the multitudinous talks of 'middlemen' about poetry is sure to be impressed by the curious fact that, in point of technique as well as of intellectual and emotional content, Hopkins is the most bafflingly 'original' of 'modern' poets though, paradoxically enough, he died nearly sixty years ago. The bulk of his poetry was written between 1876 and 1889, and committed to the care of his friend, Mr Robert Bridges, the Poet Laureate that was to be. Something or other had prevented Hopkins himself publishing his poems in his own lifetime. His longest poems had been rejected even by the Jesuit magazine, *The Month*. Unwilling to publish a scrap of his work without the knowledge of his Jesuit Superiors, but even more unwilling to seek of his own accord their consent, Hopkins left his poems in the obscurity of his note-books, grateful beyond words if a choice spirit like Bridges or Dixon read them, understood and appreciated them. In a letter to Bridges, written in 1884, Hopkins, while exonerating the Society of Jesus for not appreciating his poetry, gives a list of the people who alone had read his poems:

'Our society cannot be blamed for not valuing what it never knew of. The following are all the people I have let see my poems (not counting occasional pieces): some of them however, as you did, have shewn them to others. (1) The editor and sub-editor of our *Month* had the *Deutschland* and later the *Eurydice* offered them—(2) my father and mother and two sisters saw these, one or both of them, and I have sent them a few things besides in letters—(3) You—(4) Canon Dixon—(5) Mr Patmore—(6) Something got out about the *Deutschland* and Fr Cyprian Splaine, now of Stonyhurst, wrote to me to send it him and perhaps other poems of mine: I did so and he shewed it to others. They perhaps read it, but he afterwards acknowledged to me that in my handwriting he found it unreadable; I do not think he meant illegible—(7) On the other hand Fr Francis Bacon, a fellow novice of mine, and an admirer of my sermons, saw all and expressed a strong admiration for them which was certainly sincere. They are therefore, one may say, unknown.'[1]

When Hopkins died Bridges was by no means a famous poet; he had no doubt published a few slim volumes or 'pamphlets' of verse already, but they had brought him to the notice of only a few discriminating readers. Bridges therefore decided to bide his time. He first persuaded the editors of certain anthologies to include in them some of Hopkins's poems. In this manner eleven pieces appeared in *Poets and Poetry of the XIXth Century,* edited by A. H. Miles, with an introductory memoir on Hopkins by Bridges himself. In Beeching's *Lyra Sacra* appeared four pieces, including the now well-known 'Heaven-Haven' and 'God's Grandeur'. In the same editor's *Book of Christmas Verse* appeared the elaborate 'The Blessed Virgin compared to the Air we Breathe'.

Meanwhile some of Hopkins's letters appeared in a biography of Coventry Patmore, published at the turn of the century; and twenty years after Hopkins's death, *The Month* published a serial account of the poet's life from the pen of Fr Keating. When Bridges edited during the first World War his classic anthology, *Spirit of Man,* he included in it seven pieces of Hopkins, and among them was the opening stanza of 'The Wreck of the *Deutschland*'.[2] The

[1] *Letters,* I, pp. 196-7.
[2] ibid., Introduction, pp. xviii-xx.

curious were now getting interested in the work of Hopkins, and, having thus prepared the ground carefully, Bridges issued *Poems of Gerard Manley Hopkins*, with an adequate critical apparatus, in 1918. It was greeted in a guarded manner by the public; Mr Middleton Murry enthusiastically reviewed it in *The Nation and Athenæum*. But even a limited edition of seven hundred copies took ten years to sell. However, the 'new' poets themselves were quick to realize the significance of Hopkins. In 1930 a second edition of the *Poems*, with an Appendix of additional poems and a critical introduction, was issued by Mr Charles Williams; in the same year Fr Lahey's useful monograph on Hopkins also appeared. The publication of the three volumes of Hopkins's correspondence and of his note-books has further roused the curiosity of the 'common reader', and now, nearly sixty years after Hopkins's death, it is no exaggeration to say that he has definitely taken his rightful place in the roll-call of English poets.[3] An attempt is made in the pages that follow to give an account of Hopkins, of the man no less than of the poet, and to indicate roughly his achievements and influence in relation to the 'between the wars' period in English poetry.

[3] cf. R. G. Howarth: 'Hopkins gained a reputation, indeed ; yet he had been inadvertently cheated of his rights. . . . If his verse had been published, as was contemplated, in 1881, exerting a greater immediate influence than Whitman's it could have prevented the technical, intellectual and emotional bankruptcy represented by the lesser pieces that crowd the *Oxford Book of Victorian Verse*. It might even have convinced Browning that attempts to force speech rhythms on strong metres were against the grain. It would, indeed, have changed the whole course of English poetry.' (*Meanjin Papers*, Summer 1944, Brisbane.)

II. BOYHOOD: EARLY POEMS

THE Hopkinses of Stratford, Essex, were respectable Tories, High Church Anglicans, English to the very core. Gerard Manley Hopkins was born, the eldest of eight children, on 11 June 1844. Of his grandfather, Gerard wrote later to Bridges: 'My grandfather was a surgeon, a fellow-student of Keats', and once conveyed a body through Plymouth at the risk of his own.'[1] Hopkins's mother was a rare compound of the eternal feminine attributes of common sense and mysticism. His father, Manley Hopkins, was an indifferent poet but a very successful Consul of the Hawaiian Islands to Great Britain. Manley Hopkins published, among other works, *A Manual of Marine Insurance*, *A Handbook of Average*, and *Hawaii: an Historical Account of the Sandwich Islands*; and his *Spicilegium Poeticum* was a book of verses representing the work of about fifty years, and expressing 'several moods and feelings experienced during the changing hours of a long life'.[2] Gerard Manley Hopkins apparently inherited qualities from both his parents: 'this artistic strain in her family, and the poetical in her husband's, took deep root in the mind of their son.'[3] Besides, both his maternal and paternal uncles were painters.

Considering his antecedents, then, there was no reason at all why Gerard should not have developed in due course into a Tory diehard, sane and practical and cultured and a little complacent, and ultimately an Under Secretary in the Salisbury administration. But no, Gerard's life was star-crossed from the beginning, and ever his nature sought expression in seeming oddity, and he became consequently something of a problem to all.

[1] *Letters*, I, p. 51.   [2] ibid., p. 322.   [3] Lahey, p. 1.

Gerard had his early education at home under an aunt who knew both music and painting. The boy eagerly reacted to the world of sound and colour, and the tastes he now acquired became a part of his very being. Undoubtedly, Gerard was precocious; he was startlingly 'original' sometimes. Observant and sensitive, he found that his eye could not choose but see, his ear could not choose but hear; walking on a meadow or lost in the Hainault Forest, Gerard intently scrutinized his surroundings and attempted to take stock of Nature's myriad significances.

Presently, Gerard was put to school in the regular way; first he went to a day school in Hampstead, and later to the Grammar School at Highgate, 'a place formerly associated with such illustrious names as Lamb, Keats, Coleridge, and De Quincey'.[4] Gerard was at Highgate School for about ten years, joining it in 1854 and leaving it in 1863 for Oxford. During this important period of his life, Gerard enjoyed the friendship of other boys like E. H. Coleridge, the great poet's grandson, and one Marcus Andrew Hislop Clarke, who later distinguished himself as an Australian man of letters and became secretary of the Public Library at Melbourne. A third friend, Charles Noble Luxmoore, is one of our principal authorities concerning Gerard's adolescence. In answer to a query from Mr Arthur Hopkins, Mr Luxmoore gave this intimate account of his relations with Gerard at Highgate:

'Your brother even at that time was both popular and respected. Tenacious when duty was concerned, he was full of fun, rippling over with jokes, and chaff, facile with pencil and pen, with rhyming jibe or cartoon.... Quiet, gentle, always nice, and always doing his work well I think he must have been a charming boy from a master's point

[4] Lahey, p. 3.

of view, but he was completely changed by any wrong or ill treatment on their part.... No, your brother, as we understood him, was a quiet, gentle, upright boy, whom we loved for his consistency, his goodness & great ability .... there was no fight in him, unless he was unjustly used or attacked, and in that he was godlike, for it sprang from his love of justice, of truth.'[5]

The poet R. W. Dixon had taught at Highgate for a short time, and years later he clearly recollected Gerard Hopkins as 'a pale young boy, very light and active, with a very meditative & intellectual face'.[6]

A boy in his teens, who is godlike in his rage against injustice, and who is pale and meditative, is rather an unusual phenomenon. He thinks too much, and such men are dangerous. When Gerard was only fourteen years old, he came to the extraordinary conclusion that people drank far too much, and hence he gave up drinking, even water, for a whole week. It was no mere bravado, for he boasted of this to none, and the truth came out accidentally after he had actually carried out his resolve. On another occasion, according to Cyril Hopkins, 'Gerard discovered that every one ate too much salt at their meals, and passed a week without taking any'. From instances like these the conclusion is reached that Gerard had 'an ample supply' of moral courage, but 'there was also a vein of eccentricity in his character which somewhat marred the beauty of it, and sometimes led him into difficulties that might easily have been avoided'.[7] In the meantime Gerard accompanied his father, firstly on his tour through Belgium and the Rhineland, and, three years later, on his tour through southern

---

[5] *Letters*, III, pp. 248-9.   [6] ibid., II, p. 4.
[7] Quoted in Lahey, pp. 6-7. Also Pick: 'We are justified in saying that these acts of self-denial are indications of an early determination to master himself, of a courageous strength of will.' (*Gerard Manley Hopkins*, p. 4.)

Germany; and these journeys made a lasting impression on Gerard's impressionable mind.

While Nature, her manifold hues and sounds, fascinated young Gerard, no less did language, its semantic and phonetic import, intrigue him, hold him almost in thrall. Early he seemed to revel in the luxury of words. Did he not describe Clarke as 'a kaleidoscopic, parti-coloured, harlequinesque, thaumatropic being'?[8] Gerard was then a mere stripling of twelve and this fascination for words was to prove a life-long passion with him.

Meanwhile Gerard was writing verses with some assiduity. Some whole poems and a few fragments of this period have happily survived. Two of these, 'The Escorial' and 'A Vision of the Mermaids', were school prize poems belonging to 1860 and 1862 respectively. In 1863 he contributed to *Once A Week* a short poem entitled 'Winter with the Gulf Stream', and presently wrote to E. H. Coleridge: 'I have been writing a good deal, in poetry I mean.'[9] If he did write a 'good deal' at Highgate or just before going to Oxford, much of it is surely lost; but, perhaps, considered as sheer poetry, our loss is not much.

Of these early poems, 'Spring and Death' is cast in the form of a dream. Shelley exultingly asked, 'If Winter comes, can Spring be far behind?' And Keats moaned—

> Ay, in the very temple of Delight
>   Veil'd Melancholy has her sovran shrine,
>   Though seen of none save him whose strenuous tongue
> Can burst Joy's grape against his palate fine.

Hopkins has inverted Shelley's question and superimposed it on Keats's melancholy, and hence his 'Spring and Death' insinuates the tragic impermanence of all things beautiful—

---

[8] Lahey, p. 4.   [9] *Letters*, III, p. 6.

> As I walk'd a stilly wood,
> Sudden, Death before me stood....
> 'Death,' said I 'what do you here
> At this Spring season of the year?'
> 'I mark the flowers ere the prime
> Which I may tell at Autumn-time.'....
>   It seem'd so hard and dismal thing,
> Death, to mark them in the Spring.[10]

This is a straightforward poem, and its form is distantly reminiscent of medieval 'visions' like Langland's *Piers Plowman* and the anonymous *Pearl*.

'The Escorial', dated Easter 1860, is in fourteen Spenserian stanzas. There are in it several striking descriptions which, though they betray the influence of Byron, are certainly creditable for a lad of sixteen. The poem begins with a description of the palace of the Escorial—

> There is a massy pile above the waste
> Amongst Castilian barrens mountain-bound;
> A sombre length of grey; four towers placed
> At corners flank the stretching compass round;
> A pious work with threefold purpose crown'd—
> A cloister'd convent first, the proudest home
> Of those who strove God's gospel to confound
> With barren rigour and a frigid gloom—
> Hard by a royal palace and a royal tomb.[11]

Then follows an account of the origin of the Escorial: once 'amidst the heat of battle' Philip II 'took oath, while glory or defeat hung in the swaying of the fierce mêlée', to raise a fitting monument to St Lawrence. Philip won, and

> He rais'd the convent as a monstrous grate;
> The cloisters cross'd with equal courts betwixt
> Formed bars of stone; beyond in stiffen'd state
> The stretching palace lay as handle fix'd.[12]

[10] *Poems*, No. 75.   [11] ibid., No. 76, st. 1.
[12] ibid., st. 4.

The word-pictures that follow reveal the young poet's almost uncanny intimacy with architectural details; and so too the description of the interior of the Escorial is vivified by his ecstatic appreciation of the great masters of painting—

No finish'd proof was this of Gothic grace
With flowing tracery engemming rays
Of colour in high casements face to face;
And foliag'd crownals (pointing how the ways
Of art best follow nature) in a maze
Of finish'd diapers, that fills the eye
And scarcely traces where one beauty strays
And melts amidst another; ciel'd on high
With blazon'd groins, and crowned with hues of majesty....

The rang'd long corridors and cornic'd halls,
And damasqu'd arms and foliag'd carving piled—
With painting gleamed the rich pilaster'd walls—
There play'd the virgin mother with her Child
In some broad palmy mead, and saintly smiled,
And held a cross of flowers in purple bloom;
He, where the crownals droop'd, himself reviled
And bleeding saw.—There hung from room to room
The skill of dreamy Claude, and Titian's mellow gloom.[13]

The concluding stanzas refer to the gradual decay of the Escorial, its abandonment by the monks, its despoliation by the 'baffled Frank', and its final desolation and tragedy.

The other prize poem, 'A Vision of the Mermaids', was written towards the close of 1862, and is in heroic couplets. Already a more supple mastery of rhythm is evident, and the evocation of the mermaids is rich, sensuous and beautiful. The model is obviously Keats—especially the Keats of 'Endymion'. This is from Keats's 'Hymn to Pan'—

> O thou, for whose soul-soothing quiet, turtles
> Passion their voices cooingly 'mong myrtles,

[13] *Poems*, No. 76, st. 6 and 10.

> What time thou wanderest at eventide
> Through sunny meadows, that outskirt the side
> Of thine enmossed realms: O thou, to whom
> Broad leaved fig trees even now foredoom
> Their ripened fruitage; yellow girted bees
> Their golden honeycombs; our village leas
> Their fairest blossom'd beans and poppied corn...

And this from 'A Vision of the Mermaids'—

> And through their parting lids there came and went
> Keen glimpses of the inner firmament;
> Fair beds they seem'd of water-lily flakes
> Clustering entrancingly in beryl lakes:
> Anon, across their swimming splendour strook,
> An intense line of throbbing blood-light shook
> A quivering pennon; then, for eye too keen,
> Ebb'd back beneath its snowy lids, unseen.[14]

There is evident in these two passages the same loading of every rift with ore that Keats so much commended; and, indeed, the whole of 'A Vision of the Mermaids' is an interesting example of verbal embroidery. The very words thrill, as the poet's senses had once been thrilled by the intoxication of nature; Hopkins loves words, but this is no fraudulent love; it is born of intense living in the realms of nature and of language. Rightly Professor Abbott finds in this poem 'a native craftsmanship in the writing and a welling-up of youthful lyricism strong in promise'.[15] Passages like the following are at once surprising and satisfying in their imagery and their verbal brilliance—

> Plum-purple was the west; but spikes of light
> Spear'd open lustrous gashes, crimson-white....

> Some trail'd the Nautilus: or on the swell
> Tugg'd the boss'd, smooth-lipp'd, giant Strombus-shell.

[14] *Poems*, No. 77.
[15] *Letters*, I, Introduction, p. xxv.

> Some carried the sea-fan; some round the head
> With lace of rosy weed were chapleted;
> One bound o'er dripping gold a turquoise-gemm'd
> Circlet of astral flowerets....

There is assonance and alliteration; there is the unmistakable flair for the crucial adjective; and there is also the alert forge at work, hammering out memorable combinations like 'encrimsoning spot', 'rosy-budded fire', 'dainty-delicate fretted fringe', 'dainty onyx-coronals', and 'bubbles bugle-eyed'. Amateurish some of these artifices may be, and there may be discernible, here and there, an undesirable lushness of imagery and epithet: but the experiments clearly enough show in which direction the wind of Hopkins's poetry may in future be expected to blow. On the other hand, the following beautiful lines constitute an almost Keatsian achievement—

> But most in a half-circle watch'd the sun;
> And a sweet sadness dwelt on everyone;
> I knew not why,—but know that sadness dwells
> On Mermaids—whether that they ring the knells
> Of seamen whelm'd in chasms of the mid-main,
> As poets sing; or that it is a pain
> To know the dusk depths of the ponderous sea,
> The miles profound of solid green, and be
> With loath'd cold fishes, far from man—or what;—
> I know the sadness but the cause know not.

Another early poem, 'Winter with the Gulf Stream', is written in *terza rima* but ends with a couplet. Hopkins referred to this poem long afterwards in a letter to Bridges: 'Shelley certainly has one or more pieces in that measure printed in stanzas. . . . I borrowed also the contrivance of ending with a couplet, which has the convenience of ravelling up the rhymes. Treated in this stanza form *terza rima* is one of the simplest of measures as it is one of the most beautiful: at each stanza's end you can either rest or go on with equally charming effect.'[16] The poem was considerably revised later on, but even the original version is not without some characteristic lines like—

> Long beds I see of violets
> In beryl lakes which they reef o'er:
> A Pactolean river frets
>
> Against its tawny-golden shore:
> All ways the molten colours run:
> Till, sinking ever more and more
>
> Into an azure mist, the sun
> Drops down engulf'd, his journey done.[17]

[16] *Letters*, I, p. 142.   [17] *Letters*, III, pp. 285-6.

III. OXFORD

GERARD Hopkins certainly did not get on well with the authorities at Highgate. Dyne, the Headmaster, and Nesfield (who later wrote books on grammar, used widely even today), the assistant master, needlessly bullied the sensitive Gerard, and often drove him to desperation. Nevertheless, Gerard was a studious boy; besides the prizes he got for his poems, he was awarded a scholarship and later won an exhibition for Balliol College, Oxford. Glad to leave Highgate, but gladder still to be at Balliol, Gerard Hopkins went to Oxford in October, 1863, full of hopes and plans for the future.

The Oxford of Hopkins's day was not exactly the Oxford of Gibbon's—a grandiose school for idlers and a closed preserve for those who were willing to sign the thirty-nine Articles of the Church of England, which were then 'signed by more than read, and read by more than believed by them'. Since 1858 Oxford had ceased to be purely sectarian and Protestant; but in 1863 it was far less liberal in its outlook than it is today. Benjamin Jowett was the guiding spirit at Oxford, at any rate at Balliol; he seemed to loom immense with his vast erudition in Greek and his apparent professorial infallibility. There were others, too, in the University who then exercised considerable influence on the undergraduates. There was Walter Pater, a 'pale creature, with a large moustache', chewing the languid phrases, and 'looking out of the window at the sunset'.[1] There were Canon Liddon and Proctor Riddell and Dr Pusey, and there were tutors and preachers numberless, who exerted varying degrees of influence on the under-

---

[1] Mallock, *The New Republic*.

graduates, on their religious beliefs no less than on their studies.²

A good deal of what Lytton Strachey said about Newman seems to be applicable to Gerard Hopkins also. Hopkins, too, 'was a child of the Romantic Revival, a creature of emotion and of memory, a dreamer whose secret spirit dwelt apart in delectable mountains, an artist whose subtle senses caught, like a shower in the sunshine, the impalpable rainbow of the immaterial world. In other times, under other skies, his days would have been more fortunate. He might have helped to weave the garland of Meleager, or to mix the *lapis lazuli* of Fra Angelico, or to chase the delicate truth in the shade of an Athenian palæstra, or his hands might have fashioned those ethereal faces that smile in the niches of Chartres. Even in his own age he might, at Cambridge, whose cloisters have ever been consecrated to poetry and common sense, have followed quietly in Gray's footsteps. . . . At Oxford, he was doomed.'³ In a truer sense than is grasped by Strachey, Newman and Hopkins merely realized their potentialities, intellectually and spiritually, at Oxford.

Hopkins soon made friends at Oxford, talked and walked with them for hours on end, corresponded with them during the vacations; he also jotted down all sorts of things in his Diaries. The letters written during the early Oxford period to Alexander William Mowbray Baillie, who was to prove one of Hopkins's lifelong friends, furnish us with several hints regarding the poet's inclinations and aspira-

² cf. Pick : "There were two major streams flowing through Oxford in the 'Sixties. One was the spirit of Rationalism in religion, counteracted by a new renaissance of Tractarianism, the other was the growing Aesthetic movement. To these main streams other minor brooks were tributaries.' (p. 5.)
³ *Eminent Victorians* (Phoenix Edition), p. 13.

tions. Under date 10 July 1863, Hopkins writes to Baillie: 'I am sketching (in pencil chiefly) a good deal. . . . I think I have told you that I have particular periods of admiration for particular things in Nature; for a certain time I am astonished at the beauty of a tree, shape, effect, etc., then when the passion, so to speak, has subsided, it is consigned to my treasury of explored beauty, and acknowledged with admiration and interest ever after, while something new takes its place in my enthusiasm. The present fury is the ash, and perhaps barley and two shapes of growth in leaves and one in tree boughs and also a confirmation of fine-weather cloud.'[4] Many of the sketches Hopkins drew about this time have been beautifully reproduced by Mr Humphry House in his edition of Hopkins's miscellaneous papers and note-books.[5] In another letter to the same correspondent, Hopkins lays down, after the manner of Demosthenes, that 'the first requisite for a critic is liberality, and the second liberality, and the third, liberality'.[6] He gently remonstrates with his friend for his tacit refusal to give his opinion on Hopkins's poetry. Some months later, Hopkins writes to Baillie: 'My mother does not let me fast at all, and says I in particular must never do it again, and in fact I believe I must not. I feel like the Hindus when the Suttee was abolished.'[7] This is an alarming note; but the same letter contains a brilliant parody of Bacon and an amusing pencil sketch of Simeon the Stileite, and these, for the time being, quite reassure us.

Meanwhile Hopkins was busy, writing poetry and sketching and jotting down unusual things in his Diaries.

[4] *Letters*, III, p. 55.
[5] *The Note-Books and Papers of Gerard Manley Hopkins*, see pictures facing pp. 22, 32 and 48.
[6] *Letters*, III, p. 57.   [7] ibid., p. 60.

In a letter written in August 1864, Hopkins recounts his literary and artistic activities, and concludes: 'I hope, dear Baillie, you will not think me too egotistical in speaking thus at length and thus freely about myself and my hopes. I have now a more rational hope than before of doing something—in poetry and painting.'[8] The next letter elaborates certain notes in his Diary[9] on the three gradations of verse— poetry or the language of inspiration, Parnassian, and mere poetical language. Parnassian comes between great poetry written under the irresistible impulsion of genius and mere poetic diction made to do duty for poetry. Parnassian 'is spoken *on and from the level* of a poet's mind, not, as in the other case, where the inspiration which is the gift of genius, raises him above himself'.[10] Much of *Paradise Lost* and *Paradise Regained,* and nearly the whole of *Færie Queene* are, according to Hopkins, written in Parnassian. A letter like this not merely reveals Hopkins's constant preoccupation with the mechanism of writing verse but also his aptitude for aesthetic generalization.

Gerard Hopkins, 'the Star of Balliol',[11] was at first responsive to Jowett and was responsive too to the liberalism then prevalent at Oxford. In so far as Hopkins was an earnest student, a rational being, the scholarly Jowett stimulated him, satisfied him. But there were other cravings as well, silent, untranslatable stirrings within his breast that gave him no quiet, that insisted on self-expression, that lured him to fresh woods and pastures new. The companionship of a Ritualist by name William Addis, acting like a catalytic agent, quickened Hopkins's aesthetic pulse. There were enjoyable walks, and the enthusiastic youngsters drank the multifoliate loveliness of Nature, its elms and

[8] *Letters*, III, p. 67. [9] *Note-Books,* pp. 29-30.
[10] *Letters*, III, p. 69. [11] Jowett's phrase.

cloud effects and wild apples beautiful in blossom.
These walks, no less than travels to Nuremberg and the
Bavarian and Swiss mountains, intensified Hopkins's perception of the beautiful in Nature. In the letters written
during this period, as also in his note-books and diaries,
there are innumerable arresting images that merely want
the name of poetry and its verse form:

'Standing on a high field on all sides over the hedge the
horizon balanced its blue rim. The cowslips' heads, I see,
tremble in wind. Noticed also frequent partings of ash-
boughs.'[12]

'Feathery rows of young corn. Ruddy, furred and
branchy tops of the elms backed by rolling cloud. Frieze
of sculpture, long-membered vines tugged at by reaching
pursuant fauns, and lilies.'[13]

'The butterfly perching in a cindery dusty road and
pinching his scarlet valves. . . . Mallowy red of sunset and
sunrise clouds.'[14]

'The sun just risen
Flares his wet brilliance in the dintless heaven.'[15]

'Drops of rain hanging on rails etc seen with only the
lower rim lighted like nails (of fingers). Screws of brooks
and twines. Soft chalky look with more shadowy middles
of the globes of cloud on a night with a moon faint or
concealed.'[16]

Now and then the ideas are also given the formal
appearance of verse, as in—

> The stars were packed so close that night
>   They seemed to press and stare
>   And gather in like hurdles bright
>   The liberties of air.[17]

[12] *Note-Books*, p. 9. [13] ibid., p. 41.
[14] ibid., p. 49. [15] ibid., p. 41.
[16] ibid., p. 53. [17] ibid., p. 53.

Here and elsewhere, especially in the maturer Journals which Hopkins kept from 1868 onwards, his descriptions of Nature seem to be struggling hard to express by means of original, even startling, similitudes some fundamental, if fugitive, truths. 'Moonlight hanging or dropping on treetops like blue cobweb!' 'The foam-cuffs in the river, looked down upon, were of the crispiest endive spraying!' Are these conceits, or are they luminous images? Hopkins's concoctions are like that again and again; the similitudes are unexpected, apparently even absurd, but at length they have generally to be accepted as genuine. They are now a part of the very fabric of his thinking, of his soul's being. What, then, has happened?

Here it is necessary to digress a little. The medieval philosopher, St Bonaventure, had subtly differentiated between the primary vestiges of God's handiwork and the more integral secondary vestiges that are not so plainly visible to all. Almost any one can comprehend the material attributes of the external world; but to see into the heart of things, to apprehend the design and the purpose beneath all the apparent chaos and cruelty, to relate in the most perfect way the Creator with the Creation, to see the ordainer of all order through the very disorder surrounding us, are no easy tasks and demand greater spiritual concentration than if the poet were objectively to sing of birds and beasts and dells and dingles. St Bonaventure recognized various stages in the apprehension of ultimate reality through a study of, and a communion with, our surroundings. 'The shadow is a distant and confused representation of God; the vestige a distant but distinct representation; the image, a representation which is both distinct and close. . . . The image is therefore an analogue of the divine life, not a mere effect of God, and that is why, when it looks attentively into itself, the soul discerns a sort of reflection of the creative essence in the obscurity of its lowest depths.'[18] Hopkins, too, was fumbling thus to achieve self-expression to break through the shell of deceptive shadows and vestiges and touch the kernel of reality within. The spiritual and physical world were one, and the filiations between them, drawn in closer and ever closer harmony, would be the subject matter of Hopkins's Nature poetry and poetic prose. He felt the need to use words with new connotations; he invented new words when the existing vocabulary failed him. For instance, Hopkins explains the sense in which he would like to use the word 'sake' in a letter to Bridges: 'I mean by it the being a thing has outside itself, as a voice by its echo, a face by its reflection, a body by its shadow, a man by his name, fame, or memory, *and also* that in the thing by virtue of which especially it has this being abroad, and that is something distinctive, marked, specifically or individually speaking, as for a voice and echo clearness; for a reflected image light, brightness; for a shadow-casting body bulk; for a man genius, great achievements, amiability, and so on.'[19] In other words, 'sake' refers to the unique attribute of a thing by means of which a particular effect is produced on other things. 'Instress' and 'inscape' are two other words frequently used by Hopkins:

'All things are upheld by instress and are meaningless without it.'[20]

'The instress of its size came from comparison not with what was visible but with the remembrance of other clouds.'[21]

---

[18] Etienne Gilson, *The Philosophy of St Bonaventure*, English Translation (Sheed & Ward, 1938), pp. 211, 219.
[19] *Letters*, I, p. 83.   [20] *Note-Books*, p. 98.
[21] ibid., p. 150.

'Spanish chestnuts: their inscape here bold, jutty, somewhat oak-like, attractive, the branching visible and the leaved peaks spotted so as to make crests of eyes.'[22]

'The ashtree growing in the corner of the garden was felled. It was lopped first: I heard the sound and looking out and seeing it maimed there came at that moment a great pang and I wished to die and not to see the inscapes of the world destroyed any more.'[23]

The precise meaning of these two words cannot be explained. But it is clear enough that 'instress' signifies the design cohering the particulars of a scene, that gives each particular item a habitation and a frame of reference, while 'inscape' signifies the core of creative purposiveness underlying, and galvanizing into a spiritual entity, the formal design. 'Sake', 'instress' and 'inscape', then, are further and nearer approximations to our apprehension of ultimate reality.

Hopkins placed so much emphasis on 'instress' and 'inscape' because he thought that only in terms of these could the universe be apprehended as an ordered whole, a cosmos. Form is no futile abstraction but the concrete pattern within whose frames of reference the particulars, the objective vestiges and signs and the details of diction and technique, may establish a condition of stable equilibrium. As Mr Edward Watkin has pointed out, the 'matter' and 'form' of an object refer respectively to its particularity (thisness) and character (thusness): 'the matter changes in so far as it assumes different forms. It can assume one form or another. That is to say *matter is the potentiality or potency of receiving form.*'[24] The form remains, the function never dies; the One remains, though the many

---

[22] *Note-Books*, p. 108. [23] ibid., p. 174.
[24] *A Philosophy of Form* (Sheed & Ward, 1935), p. 9.

change and pass. Form is thus the underlying unity, the 'instress' that integrates the diversities and mutations in matter; form is eternal, and transcends the dichotomies that at first baffle our understanding, but matter is fluctuating, shifting, dying, and constantly being reborn. What then? 'In so far as we apprehend form, we apprehend truth and our judgements are true. And progress in knowledge of truth is twofold. The more fully we apprehend a form, the fuller our knowledge of objects which embody it; and the higher and more comprehensive the forms we know (that is to say, the closer they participate in and approach to the Absolute Form) the more adequate, or rather the less inadequate, our knowledge of reality, of objective truth. As form is the principle and therefore the measure of intelligibility, that is to say of *objective* truth, our apprehension of form is the measure of our knowledge, the measure of *subjective* truth.'[25] In trying always, in prose or in poetry, in meditation or in utterance, to reach and hold fast to the 'instress' of a scene or of an episode, and to justify the 'inscape' as part of a providential scheme, in attempting thus to paint the design and hymn the harmony inherent in the nature of things, Hopkins was at once a true poet of Nature and a member of the Church Militant justifying the ways of God to men. Chastened by the deep power of joy that comes from such ecstatic communion with Nature, Hopkins could now write in his Diary—

'I have found the dominant of my range and state—
Love, O my God, to call Thee Love and Love.'[26]

[25] *A Philosophy of Form*, pp. 69-70.
[26] *Note-Books*, p. 53.

IV. CONVERSION

MEANWHILE Hopkins the undergraduate was not idle. He was reading incessantly, intensively, and his reading ranged from literature to architecture, Church History to philosophy. He contemplated writing an essay on *Some Aspects of Modern Mediævalism*—'title not such as might be wished, but represents pictorially what is meant'.[1] He read desultorily the works of contemporaries like Dixon, the Brownings, the Rossettis; he presently made a memorandum that he should read Gray, *Vanity Fair*, several of Shakespeare's plays, Max Muller's *The Christians of St Thomas*, Gresley's *Short Treatise on the English Church*[2]— what an assortment! In spite of his excursions into regions not falling strictly within an average student's domain, Hopkins got a first class in Classical Moderations in Michaelmas, 1864. To Baillie he wrote later, in answer to a letter of congratulation: 'I have had many letters of congratulation, and have fallen into that state which comes when you have thought or heard a great deal about something that has happened to you—that you have to make an effort to think what the original cause of all the consequences was. With a Fal la la la la.'[3]

But this exultation was to be short-lived. Something disturbing and strange was happening to Hopkins on the spiritual plane. His religious opinions and convictions, his very faith and what it fed on, were undergoing a rapid transformation. The Oxford of Hopkins's day had already sustained several cracks in the outwardly rigid Protestant

---

[1] *Note-Books*, p. 21.   [2] ibid., p. 28.
[3] *Letters*, III, p. 76.

framework. The agitations of the Tractarian movement
had calmed down a little, but the Puseyites were still there,
and Dr Newman himself was not so very far off![4] Hopkins
was inevitably caught in the obscure spiritual eddies of
Oxford and helplessly found himself drifting—he did not
know whither.

Let us follow, as far as we may, the involutions of his
mind and the changing convictions of his anguished soul.
On 25 March 1865, Hopkins 'confessed' to Canon Liddon.
During a walking tour in the summer of the same year
Hopkins and Addis (according to the latter) 'walked out to
the Benedictine Monastery at Belmont and had a long conversation with Canon Ranyal, afterwards Abbot. I think he
made a great impression on both of us and I believe that
from that time our faith in Anglicanism was really gone.'[5]
About the middle of September, 1865, Hopkins wrote to
Baillie:

'You will no doubt understand what I mean by saying
that the *sordidness* of things, wh. one is compelled perpetually to feel, is perhaps . . . the most unmixedly painful
thing one knows of: and this is (objectively) intensified and
(subjectively) destroyed by Catholicism. If people cd. all
know this, to take no higher ground, no other inducement
wd. to very many minds be needed to lead them to Catholicism and no opposite inducement cd. dissuade them from it.'[6]

Already, then, Hopkins had not merely abandoned the
Anglican position, but was fast gravitating towards Catholicism.

But hesitations and doubts as to his immediate duty
were still there. In October 1865, Hopkins made this entry
in his Diary: 'Note that if ever I should leave the English

---

[4] Newman's masterpiece, *Apologia Pro Vita Sua*, was
published in 1864.
[5] Quoted in Lahey, p. 24. [6] *Letters*, III, pp. 79-80.

Church the fact of Provost Fortescue is to be got over.'⁷ But he continued his austerities and experiments in the mortification of the physical body: 'For Lent. No pudding on Sundays. No tea except if to keep me awake and then without sugar. Meat only once a day. No verses in Passion Week or on Fridays. Not to sit in armchair except can work in no other way. Ash Wednesday and Good Friday bread and water.'⁸

As the year 1866 advanced, Hopkins's views gradually crystallized. He told himself that he would become a Catholic; told others—a few intimates—to that effect, as if to nerve himself to the great adventure. His Oxford friend, William Alexander Macfarlane, made this note in his Diary, under date 24 July: 'Walked out with Hopkins and he confided to me his fixed intention of going over to Rome. I did not attempt to argue with him as his grounds did not admit of argument.'⁹

What was Hopkins to do then? He decided to consult the greatest English Catholic then living, a convert and an Oxonian like himself—Dr Newman.¹⁰ On 28 August 1866, Hopkins wrote from his parental home, Oak Hill, Hampstead, to Dr Newman, at the Oratory at Birmingham: '... I do not want to be helped to any conclusions of belief, for I am thankful to say my mind is made up, but the necessity of becoming a Catholic ... coming upon me suddenly has put me into painful confusion of mind about my immediate duty in my circumstances.'¹¹

⁷ *Note-Books*, p. 52.   ⁸ ibid., p. 53.
⁹ *Letters*, III, p. 250.
¹⁰ Pick, '... there is every reason to believe that Hopkins's path had been Newman's path, for he read *Difficulties of Anglicans* with great interest during his days at Oxford and years later he wanted to edit his *Grammar of Assent* with notes and a commentary.' (p. 18.)   ¹¹ *Letters*, III, p. 11.

In other words, Hopkins wished to consult Newman as to when precisely he might be received into the Catholic Church. A meeting was arranged, and presumably it quietened Hopkins's agitations. He alludes to the meeting in a letter to Robert Bridges, written on 22 September 1866:

'Dr Newman was most kind, I mean in the very best sense, for his manner is not that of solicitous kindness but genial and almost, so to speak, unserious. And if I may say so, he was so sensible. He asked questions which made it clear for me how to act; I will tell you presently what that is: he made sure I was acting deliberately and wished to hear my arguments; when I had given them and said I cd. see no way out of them, he laughed and said "Nor can I": and he told me I must come to the church to accept and believe—as I hope I do . . . in no way did he urge me on, rather the other way.'[12]

About the same time, Hopkins wrote to another of his Oxford friends, the Rev. E. W. Urquhart: 'By mercy of God I am a penitent waiting for admission to the Catholic Church. . . . Now I may speak plainly: I have been for about two months a convert to the Church of Christ and am hoping to be received early next term: I most earnestly hope you will delay no longer.'[13] With the proverbial zeal of the recent convert, Hopkins is here 'earnestly' hoping that Mr Urquhart will also become a Catholic. He wrote again, shortly afterwards: 'I hope the painful time of yr. hesitation may be short.'[14] Mr Urquhart apparently did not like these importunities, for almost immediately afterwards we find Hopkins writing: 'It was certainly wrong of me to be so much in a hurry about you.'[15] As for Hopkins himself, the die was definitely cast. He informed one friend

---

[12] *Letters*, I, p. 5.   [13] *Letters*, III, p. 13.
[14] ibid., p. 16.   [15] ibid., p. 17.

after another, and then his parents, about the step he proposed to take.

As might be expected, Hopkins's decision stunned his parents on the one hand and his former associates, the Ritualists, on the other. From Oxford Hopkins wrote to Newman, shaken to the depths: 'I have been up at Oxford just long enough to have heard fr. my father and mother in return for my letter announcing my conversion. Their answers are terrible: I cannot read them twice. If you will pray for them and me just now I shall be deeply thankful.'[16] Dr Pusey, in reply to a respectful request for interview, wrote sharply: 'Those who will gain by what you seem determined to do, will be the unbelievers.'[17] Canon H. P. Liddon, on the contrary, bombarded Hopkins with moving entreaties, hoping against hope that they might produce the desired effect: 'I do entreat you to pause.' Again: 'I cannot tell you how earnestly I trust that Our Lord will keep you from making a very serious mistake indeed.' And lastly: 'I can hardly help hoping that you *may* have delayed taking the final & fatal step. . . . Do have the courage—to stop—even now.'[18]

Hopkins's mind was in turmoil, but more than ever he was convinced of the imperative spiritual necessity of the step he proposed to take. Newman, of course, was a vast consoling factor, for he wrote understandingly: 'It is not wonderful that you should not be able to take so great a step without trouble and pain.'[19] Hopkins could wait no longer; on 21 October 1866, he embraced the Catholic faith, and bravely braced himself to face an almost alien world. As the days—and the weeks—passed, the clouds drifted away, and the sky seemed to clear a little. Within

[16] *Letters*, III, p. 19.
[17] ibid., p. 253.
[18] ibid., pp. 253, 255, 256.
[19] ibid., p. 20.

a month or two, Hopkins found himself on easier terms
than he had expected with his friends and relations at home;
he actually contemplated spending the Christmas vacation
with his parents.[20] Nevertheless, Dr Newman invited
Hopkins to spend some little time at the Birmingham
Oratory: 'I want to see you for the pleasure of seeing you—
but, besides that, I think it good that a recent convert should
pass some time in a religious house, to get into Catholic
ways.'[21] Hopkins was eager to go, but was at first apprehensive lest the plan should cause pain to his parents at home;[22]
eventually, however, he went, and was received very kindly
at the Oratory.

Returning to Oxford, Hopkins threw himself into his
studies, and obtained a first in Greats in the Spring of 1867.
He then spent the Easter at the Benedictine Priory near
Hereford—'a delightful place in every way'.[23] Meanwhile
he was offered the post of a teacher by one Mr Darnell. On
communicating this news to Dr Newman, Hopkins received
an unexpected reply: 'When you said you disliked schooling, I said not a word. Else, I should have asked you to
come here for *the very purpose* for which Mr Darnell wishes
for you. . . . Since then it was only delicacy which prevented
my speaking when you were here, I have no hesitation in
asking you to accept the invitation which we now make to
you. You will find it much better for you to be in a religious house, than with Mr Darnell in the country.'[24]
Hopkins gratefully accepted the offer and went to the
Oratory on 17 September 1867.

Hopkins could now enjoy at long last some real peace
of mind. The spiritual thunderstorms had subsided and

[20] *Letters*, III, p. 257. [21] ibid., p. 258.
[22] *Letters*, I, p. 15.   [23] *Letters*, III, p. 26.
[24] ibid., p. 259.

he had sailed into the haven of bounty unscathed. The thought of Greats, too, that had long weighed 'like a millstone' round his neck,[25] had resolved itself in complete triumph and brought him relief. He was a teacher, enjoying the company of eager boys and living with Dr Newman himself. A tone of quiet happiness is perceptible in the letters written at this time. He wrote to Bridges, for instance, under date 1 November 1867: 'I am very fond of my boys and as there is nothing but boys visible that is really saying everything there is to be said about the general pleasantness of the place. I have taken to playing football but got lamed to some degree by a kick on the ancle. I have also begun the violin. . . .'[26] Hopkins taught at the Oratory, not only Latin and Greek, but also natural history in an unofficial manner; occasionally he even delighted his students by 'catching frogs and newts'.[27] After spending the Christmas vacation at Oak Hill, with his parents, Hopkins returned to the Oratory in February, 1868.

[25] *Letters*, I, p. 18.   [26] ibid., p. 18.   [27] Lahey, p. 47 n.

V. OXFORD POETRY

Of Hopkins's friends at Oxford we have already referred to Bridges, Addis, Macfarlane, Baillie and Urquhart. There was also Digby Mackworth Dolben, one of the many 'inheritors of unfulfilled renown' in English literature; Gerard Hopkins met him for the first and last time in February 1865, but even so 'conceived a high admiration for him, and always spoke of him afterwards with great affection'.[1] Dolben, like Hopkins, experienced a deep spiritual unrest and, had not death intervened, he might have become a Catholic in due course. His death by drowning was a profound shock to his friends. Hopkins wrote to Bridges in moving terms: 'You know there can very seldom have happened the loss of so much beauty (in body and mind and life) and of the promise of still more as there has been in his case—seldom I mean, in the whole world, for the conditions wd. not easily come together. . . . I want to know whether his family think of gathering and publishing, or at least printing, his poetry.'[2] This was eventually done by Bridges himself.

It is difficult now to determine exactly the full potential of Hopkins's affection for Dolben. A sonnet written shortly after their only meeting seems to have been inspired by Dolben's personality. Hopkins had bombarded Dolben with letters, but had received not 'a whiff of answer';[3] perhaps, this stirred Hopkins to write—

> Where art thou friend, whom I shall never see,
> Conceiving whom I must conceive amiss? . . .

---

[1] *The Poems of D. M. Dolben* (2nd Edition, 1915), Memoir by Robert Bridges, p. lxxiii.
[2] *Letters*, I, pp. 16-17.   [3] ibid., p. 1.

Oh! even for the weakness of the plea
That I have taken to plead with,—if the sound
Of God's dear pleadings have as yet not moved thee,—
And for those virtues I in thee have found,
Who say that had I known I had approved thee,—
For these, make all the virtue to abound,—
No, but for Christ who hath foreknown and
          loved thee.[4]

After Dolben's death, Hopkins gave expression to the poignancy of his regret in the verses he wrote in June 1868—this, at any rate, is Father Lahey's opinion. The following stanzas may appropriately be quoted here—

> My dreams were of our holy love,
> The sweet communion heart to heart.
> We had bright hopes of earthly bliss
> And never dreamt that we must part. . . .
>
> And thus I pondered wond'ring much
> While I looked up with longing eyes
> If my blue sky could be like his
> There where he rests, in Paradise.
>
> 'Tis but a little while to moan,
> 'Tis but a little time to weep,
> Till God shall say: It is enough
> And then I too may fall asleep.[5]

Once again, seven years afterwards, during a Retreat, the memory of Dolben brought Hopkins a strange illumination, and he noted in his Journal: 'I received as I think a great mercy about Dolben.'[6]

This is the proper place to consider and assess the importance of the poems and poetical fragments that Hopkins produced during the entire Oxford period. Besides the few pieces published in the standard edition of the *Poems*, several hundred verses have been included by

---

[4] *Note-Books*, p. 42.   [5] Lahey, pp. 30-32.
[6] *Note-Books*, p. 182.

Mr Humphry House in his edition of Hopkins's Note-Books and miscellaneous papers. It is impossible to estimate how much of the poetry written during the Oxford period was destroyed by Hopkins when he became a Jesuit. But the material that has happily been rescued by Mr House is sufficient to give an adequate idea of the restlessness, genuineness, and variety of Hopkins's poetic activity.

'Pilate' is a fairly long poem, written probably in 1864. It has brisk and interesting lines like—

> There is a day of all the year
> When life revisits me nerve and vein.
> They all come here and stand before me clear
> I try the Christus o'er again.
> Sir! Christ! against this multitude I strain—
> Lord, but they cry so loud. And what am I?
> And all in one say 'Crucify!'[7]

Another long poem, or rather a series of fragments held together by a common impulsion of utterance, is 'A Voice from the World', 'with which I am at present in the fatal condition of satisfaction'.[8] Intended as an answer to Christina Rossetti's 'Convent Threshold', Hopkins's verses have a more masculine vigour; and there are several animated and agonizing lines—

> The love of women is not so strong,—
> 'Tis falsely given—as love in men;
> A thing that weeps, enduring long:
> But mine is dreadful leaping pain,
> Phrenzy, but edged and clear of brain
> Ruinous heart-beat, wandering, death.
> I walk towards eve our walks again;
> When lily-yellow is the west,
> Say, o'er it hangs a water-cloud
> And ravell'd into strings of rain. . . .[9]

---

[7] *Note-Books*, pp. 13-14.   [8] *Letters*, III, p. 66
[9] *Note-Books*, p. 17.

Many more fragments follow, including a fairly continuous poem entitled 'A Soliloquy of one of the spies left in the Wilderness'; there are beautiful stray lines, some arresting stanzas, ample raw material for poetry and poetic passages, but no finished and flawless poem. There is a quotable poetic asseveration—

> Of virtues I most warmly bless,
> Most rarely seen, Unselfishness.
> And to put graver sins aside,
> I own a preference for Pride.[10]

Then follows an annihilating couplet about 'Modern Poets'—

> Our swans are now of such remorseless quill,
> Themselves live singing and their hearers kill.[11]

Then, of a sudden, two lines of exquisite Nature description—

> So late the hoar green chestnut breaks a bud,
> And feeds new leaves upon the winds of Fall. . . .[12]

'The Queen's Crowning' is written in ballad form and consists of thirty-nine stanzas. The story is told in a straightforward manner, and the dialogue is effective. The final conversation between the lovers is a moving piece of writing—

> 'Is it a lily in your hand,
>   Is it a rose I see?
> Did you pull it in the king's garden
>   When you came forth for me?'

---

[10] *Note-Books*, p. 28.   [11] ibid., p. 29.   [12] ibid., p. 31.

> 'I did not pull it in the king's garden
>   When I came forth for thee.
> If it were a flower of Paradise,
>   It were more like to be.' . . .
>
> The more she asked, the more he spoke,
>   The fairer waxèd he.
> The more he told, the less she spoke,
>   The wanner wanèd she . . .
>
> He gave her kisses cold as ice;
>   Down upon ground fell she.
> She has gone with him to Paradise.
>   There shall her crowning be.[13]

Had this poem been revised by the maturer Hopkins, as for instance 'Rest'[14] was, it too might have become a favourite anthology piece. On the other hand, the following lines clearly anticipate the later Hopkins—

Boughs being pruned, birds preenèd, show more fair;
  To grace them spires are shaped with corner squinches;
Enrichèd posts are chamfer'd; everywhere
  He heightens worth who guardedly diminishes;
Diamonds are better cut; who pare, repair . . .[15]

The artifices of assonance, alliteration, internal rhyming, and wrenched accent are all here in evidence.

Some of the other fragments given by Mr House—'Richard' and 'Floris in Italy' for example—do not call for any special comment. The sonnets relating to Hopkins's spiritual crisis are however a different matter altogether. They are odd pages violently torn from Hopkins's spiritual autobiography. The whole man—anguished and struggling and failing and yet firmly hoping—is here attempting to

---

[13] *Note-Books*, p. 38.   [14] ibid., p. 27.
[15] ibid., pp. 39-40.

articulate his soul's travail. These sonnets may not be perfect artistically, but they are indispensable to an understanding of the poet's mind during the great crisis in his early manhood. This is the third sonnet in the series which has the common title 'The Beginning of the End'—

> You see that I have come to passion's end.
> This means you need not fear the storms, the cries,
> That gave you vantage when you would despise:
> My bankrupt heart has no more tears to spend.
> Else, I am well assured I should offend
> With fiercer weepings of these desperate eyes
> For love's poor failure than his hopeless rise.
> But now I am so tired I soon shall send
> Barely a sigh in thinkings of things gone.
> Is this made plain? What have I come across
> That here will serve me for comparison?
> The sceptic disappointment and the loss
> A boy feels when the poet he pores upon
> Grows less and less sweet to him without cause.[16]

The two sonnets 'To Oxford', originally sent to Addis, are song-offerings affirming Hopkins's undying fealty to his Alma Mater. 'Easter Communion', the sonnet that follows, is an effusion ending with the affirmation, 'Lo, God shall strengthen all the feeble knees'.[17] The last sonnet given by Mr House is also gnarled by Hopkins's religious probings and self-torturings, and it bitterly regrets 'the waste done in unreticent youth which makes so small the promise' that the future holds.[18] With his decision to embrace Catholicism, of course, these intellectual and emotional eddies gradually gave place to a spiritual calm.

We shall now refer briefly to the more finished pieces of Hopkins's Oxford period, almost all being more or less

---

[16] *Note-Books*, pp. 43-4.   [17] ibid., p. 47.   [18] ibid., p. 47.

direct translations of his spiritual experiences or beliefs.
'Summa' is a flawless jewel—

> The best ideal is the true
> And other truth is none.
> All glory be ascribèd to
> The holy Three in One.[19]

Not less beautiful, though slightly more elaborate, is 'Heaven-Haven', purporting to be the utterance of a nun who takes the veil—

> I have desired to go
> Where springs not fail,
> To fields where flies no sharp and sided hail
> And a few lilies blow. . . .[20]

The exquisiteness of the last two lines is a haunting thing and recalls the first stanza of Yeats's 'The Lake Isle of Innisfree'. 'For a Picture of St Dorothea' is an honest piece of work, but its twisted rhythm and syntax mar the urgency of its vision and the directness of its communication. Artifices and rhythmic jerks are not blended into superior art, and hence we have lines like—

> O should it then be quenchèd not?
> In starry water-meads they drew
> These drops: which be they? stars or dew? . . .

But the concluding lines ring true—

> Sphered so fast, sweet soul?—We see
> Nor fruit, nor flowers, nor Dorothy.[21]

By far the most remarkable of these early poems, however, is 'The Habit of Perfection'.[22] It is simple, sensuous,

[19] *Poems*, No. 52.   [20] ibid., No. 2.
[21] ibid., No. 1.   [22] ibid., No. 3.

and is transfigured by an intense unearthly longing. We may suppose that it was written when Hopkins had no further doubts as to where his only consistent position in religion lay—when he had even dimly imagined himself in the role of a Jesuit. The poem is therefore another leaf from Hopkins's autobiography. The hesitations and mental insurrections over, Hopkins could with an easy mind now consecrate his life to a career of silent service—

> Elected Silence, sing to me
> And beat upon my whorlèd ear,
> Pipe me to pastures still and be
> The music that I care to hear.

The following is, perhaps, an anticipation of his later resolve to write no more poems—

> Shape nothing, lips; be lovely-dumb:
> It is the shut, the curfew sent
> From there where all surrenders come
> Which only makes you eloquent.

Let the eyes be shelled with double dark, may the palate yearn for no earthly wine, may the incense-breathing nostrils and the feel-of-primrose hands alike await a more ethereal wafture and a more unblemished softness from Heaven. And—

> . . . Poverty, be thou the bride
> And now the marriage feast begun,
> And lily-coloured clothes provide
> Your spouse not laboured-at nor spun.

The craving for a drawing-in of one's powers the better to achieve an intense other-worldliness is none the less commu-

nicated with a sensuous imagery reminiscent of Keats: and
the underlying idea is distantly paralleled in a rhapsody of
a Kannada mystic of the twelfth century—

> Were I lame, O Lord,
> My feet will never go astray;
> Were I blind,
> Nothing will envenom my sight;
> Were I deaf,
> No words will my ears profane;
> May I seek, then, no other refuge,
> Than your devotee's feet,
> O Lord, Kudala Sangama! [23]

'The Habit of Perfection', in its intention and its execution,
rightly ranks among the most satisfactory of Hopkins's minor
poems.[24]

Of the remaining poems of the Oxford period, none
can be said to transport the reader. Robert Bridges dismissed them as 'attempts at lyrical poems, mostly sentimental aspects of death',[25] and did not print them in his
edition of Hopkins's poems; they are, however, included
in the more recent edition issued by Mr Charles Williams.
Pieces like 'Barnfloor and Winepress', 'The Nightingale'
and 'Nondum' seem rather wooden for all their careful
phrasing and clear-spun thread of underlying thought. Now

---

[23] *Musings of Basava*, by S. S. Basawanal and K. R. Srinivasa Iyengar, p. 62.

[24] Dr Pick's comments on Hopkins's Oxford poetry are characteristic: 'The difficulty of the artist and the religious takes an enigmatic form ; the sensuous beauty of the world attracts the artist . . . . on the other hand, his religious asceticism makes him reject the senses. And the deficiencies of his undergraduate poetry, both secular and religious, may largely be told in terms of this conflict.' (p. 16.)

[25] *Poems*, p. 101.

and then we find the lines echoing our own thoughts and feelings—

> We guess; we clothe Thee, unseen King,
> With attributes we deem are meet;
> Each in his own imagining
> Sets up a shadow in thy seat;
> Yet know not how our gifts to bring,
> Where seek thee with unsandalled feet.[26]

Again, one can appreciate a stanza like the following, which tries to evoke the curious feeling produced on the poet by the music of the nightingale—

> I thought the air must cut and strain
> The windpipe when he sucked his breath
> And when he turned it back again
>   The music must be death.
> With not a thing to make me fear,
> A singing bird in morning clear
> To me was terrible to hear.[27]

But lines like—

> Terrible fruit was on the tree
> In the Acre of Gethsemane;
> For us by Calvary's distress
> The wine was rackèd from the press;
>   Now in our Altar vessels stored
> Is the sweet Vintage of our Lord.[28]

do not move us as sheer lyrical cries; their appeal depends, on the other hand, on the identity of the reader's religious beliefs with those of the poet. It is not that religious belief cannot be authentic subject matter for poetry. Dante and Homer and Milton have made religion the very stuff of their poetry, and a Hindu or a Muslim or a Catholic can read

---

[26] *Poems*, No. 80.   [27] ibid., No. 79.   [28] ibid., No. 78.

them as poets and hold them in veneration. For, in the process of poetic creation, these great poets have transfigured individual faiths and theological dogmas into the current coin of eternal verities. And such is the magic of the words and the singular potency of their movement that they induce even in a sceptical reader 'a willing suspension of disbelief'. And this too is precisely what Hopkins himself did in his successful religious hymns and in the longer poems of his maturity.

VI. THE LURE OF LOYOLA

HOPKINS was a Catholic, but that was not to be the logical conclusion of the indistinct cravings and eccentric doings of his boyhood. The melancholy and meditative lad, tortured by doubts and stray spasms of despair, by the palpable inconsistencies of the Thirty-nine Articles of the Anglican Church, had no doubt found a haven of refuge in the Church of Rome. But Hopkins loved action too, and wished to express himself in disciplined and stern endeavour; he yearned to labour hard and suffer for his Church. Hopkins was, indeed, the 'nineteenth-century English Don Quixote';[1] he would be a Christian Knight-errant, a soldier in Christ's Army, and he would dedicate his life, the resources of his intellect and spirit, to the exaltation of the power and glory of God. In other words, Hopkins decided to become a Jesuit.

On 7 February 1868 Newman wrote to Hopkins: 'You need not make up your mind till Easter comes, as we shall be able to manage matters whether you stay, or we have the mishap to lose you.'[2] Apparently, Hopkins had not returned to the Oratory after the Christmas vacation, and was feeling undecided about his future course of action. Within a few days, Hopkins had not only returned to the Oratory, but had also definitely made up his mind: for, on the 12th of February, Hopkins wrote to Baillie from the Oratory:

'I must say that I am very anxious to get away from this place. I have become very weak in health and do not

---

[1] Daniel Sargent, *Four Independents* (Sheed & Ward, 1935) p. 117.   [2] *Letters*, III, p. 260.

seem to recover myself here or likely to do so. Teaching is very burdensome, especially when you have much of it: I have . . . The boys are very nice indeed. I am expecting to take orders and soon, but I wish it to be secret till it comes about. Besides that it is the happiest and best way it practically is the only one. You know I once wanted to be a painter. But even if I could I wd. not I think, now, for the fact is that the higher and more attractive parts of the art put a strain upon the passions which I shd. think it unsafe to encounter. I want to write still and as a priest I very likely can do that too, not so freely as I shd. have liked, *e.g.*, nothing or little in the verse way, but no doubt what wd. best serve the cause of religion. But if I am a priest it will cause my mother, or she says it will, great grief and this preys on my mind very much and makes the near prospect quite black.'[3]

This was another, though a lesser, crisis in his life; once again the 'genius and mortal instruments were in council'; once again a battle was raging within the regions of the invisible, his sensuous adoration of animate nature and his human, filial emotions being pitted against the irrevocable resolve to join the army of Loyola, to 'scorn delights and live laborious days'. Hopkins had no doubts whatsoever about the rightness of his choice; at the same time, being human like any one else, he was forced to look at the immediate future with some misgivings.

In the same letter, Hopkins asked Baillie if any temporary tutorship could be made available as a stop-gap. Hopkins left the Oratory soon, and shifted for himself for some time. He would become a Jesuit later in the year, but what was he to do in the meantime? And what if he should find the life of a Jesuit a tough proposition at close quarters? He confided to Newman his resolve as well as his fears. Newman's answer was characteristic: 'I am both

[3] *Letters*, III, pp. 84-5.

surprised and glad at your news. If all is well, I wish (to) say a Mass for your perseverance. I think it is the very thing for you.... Don't call "the Jesuit discipline hard", it will bring you to heaven.'[4] This was most encouraging, and brought Hopkins considerable solace: we find him writing on 13 June to the Rev. Urquhart: 'About the end of the month I am going to Switzerland for a month.... and when I return shall be admitted at once to the Jesuit noviciate at Roehampton. It is enough to say that the sanctity has not departed fr. the order to have a reason for joining it. Since I made up my mind to this I have enjoyed the first complete peace of mind I have ever had. I am quite surprised .... at the kind and contented way my parents have come to take the prospect.'[5]

And, yet, a minor worry remained. Hopkins would like to see Switzerland before he entered the noviciate, but funds were lacking. 'In the stress of circumstance,' he writes to Fr Ignatius Ryder, 'I began writing an article for a review .... The worst is that an article must be (*i*) written, (*ii*) accepted—the first requires time, of which I have so little and perseverance of which I have none at all; the second is doubtful .... Shd. you not feel it painful to write for money? I know someone who writes newspaper articles and says it is rather depressing. Still I shd. like to sing my dying-swan-song.'[6] Fortunately for him, neither then nor later was Hopkins compelled to write for a living. He made a tour of Switzerland in due course and returned to England, both refreshed and determined to pursue his new vocation with single-hearted devotion. He came to the conclusion that the writing of poetry ill assorted with the life of a Jesuit, and, in a mood of self-immolation, destroyed much

---

[4] *Letters*, III, p. 261. [5] ibid., pp. 36-7.
[6] ibid., p. 39.

of what he had written. On 7 August, he wrote to Bridges: 'I cannot send my 'Summa' for it is burnt[7] with my other verses: I saw they would interfere with my state and vocation. I kept however corrected copies of some things which you have....'[8] In another letter, written to Canon Dixon ten years later, Hopkins wrote: 'What I had written I burnt before I became a Jesuit and resolved to write no more, as not belonging to my profession, unless it were by the wish of my superiors.'[9] Thus relieving himself, as far as it was humanly possible, of the earth-crust, Hopkins entered the Jesuit noviciate at Roehampton in September 1868.

This was no ordinary change.[10] Gerard Hopkins, a fastidious Englishman punctilious about his dress, his individuality, even his eccentricity, was a novice now, and took only two suits of clothes in his kit when he left for Roehampton. Nor did he flinch when the Jesuit uniform imposed on him the uncomfortable 'community socks'. Before they take their final vows, the Jesuits have to undergo a stiff spiritual training; and this ordeal is divided into two parts. But the period of training may extend to anything from three to fifteen years. It is impossible for a non-Catholic, indeed for any one who is not a Jesuit himself, fully to understand the nature or appreciate the efficacy of these spiritual exercises. It is said that the long retreat, the thirty days of spiritual exercises, the spiritual exercises

---

[7] No. 52 in *Poems* gives only the first four lines of a much longer poem destroyed by Hopkins in 1868.
[8] *Letters*, I, p. 24.   [9] *Letters*, II, p. 14.
[10] cf. Pick: 'It is the great dividing point of his life. On one side is the unformed youth, on the other is the Jesuit priest. On the one side is his early verse, on the other is his great poetry. In September, 1868, when Hopkins at the age of twenty-four entered the Jesuit noviciate, the entire direction of his life was changed.' (*Gerard Manley Hopkins*, p. 1.)

THE LURE OF LOYOLA 45

of St Ignatius, are all so designed as to make the young novice a true servant of God, imbued with the unbending determination to work for the greater glory of God in whatever situation He, acting through the superiors in the Order, may choose to place him. The true Jesuit is essentially a man of action—a man of deeds and not alone of words. Father Holt in *Henry Esmond* does not exaggerate very much when he rhapsodically speaks of the

> 'Society of Jesus, which numbers in its troops the greatest heroes the world ever knew:—warriors brave enough to dare or endure anything, to encounter any odds, to die any death;—soldiers that have won triumphs a thousand times more brilliant than those of the greatest General; that have brought nations on their knees to their sacred banner, the Cross; that have achieved glories and palms incomparably brighter than those awarded to the most splendid earthly conquerors—crowns of immortal light and seats in the high places of heaven.'[11]

The mission may have to be organized in strange, perhaps even alien, surroundings; a great educational institution or hospital may have to be raised; a prolonged battle may have to be waged against various disruptive forces lest the established order should totter and disintegrate into atoms; and, in more humble spheres, funds may have to be collected, corn gathered from the fields, building operations to be superintended, printing work or automobile repairs to be supervised; nay, the very floors may have to be scrubbed, the food cooked, and the clothes washed—and however exalted or humble the post of duty, however congenial or killing the nature of the work, the Jesuit should unmurmuringly answer the call, and make good. It is difficult, so very difficult, to cease to live for oneself, and to learn rather

[11] Thackeray, *Henry Esmond* (Everymans Edition), p. 348.

to live with seven-fold vigour and determination for the sake of an Order, an abstract principle. A long and stiff probation is necessary to fit a man to be a Jesuit. And hence St Ignatius Loyola has prescribed for the novices of his Order certain 'community reflections'. Mr Watkin has truly remarked that 'without a basis of contemplation, no action is possible'.[12] The Jesuits, too, before they are launched on their unflinching and unblemished career of active service are made to acquire the necessary integrity, concentration and discipline through a stringent course of contemplative spiritual exercises. In successive weeks the Jesuit novice meditates on his palpable disservice to his Creator so far, on the varied lineaments in the life story of Jesus Christ, on the supreme Mercy and Passion of the crucifixion, on the final triumph of Jesus and His glory for ever. As Fr Pollen remarks in the *Catholic Encyclopaedia*: 'In accordance with the ideals set forth in these exercises, of disinterested conformity with God's will, and of personal love of Jesus Christ, the novice is trained diligently in a meditative study of the truths of religion, in the habit of self-knowledge, in a constant scrutiny of his motives and of the actions inspired by them, in the correction of every form of self-deceit, illusion, plausible pretext, and in the education of his will, particularly in making choice of what seems best after careful deliberation and without self-seeking.'[13] During these weeks of prolonged meditation, 'the novice does not choose his own reveries. He thinks as all men—so St Ignatius held—must at times think'.[14] Since these reflections run in a particular groove, they can be stigmatized as being 'stereotyped'; and

---

[12] *A Philosophy of Form*, p. 72.
[13] Quoted in *Note-Books*, pp. 446-7.
[14] Sargent, *Four Independents*, p. 137.

not unnaturally they help to make the Jesuits a distinct and distinctive Order. They wear the same long, flowing uniforms, and often we cannot tell one Jesuit from another. Unless one has moved with a Jesuit pretty closely—and not always even then—it is not easy to form any adequate idea of even the major contours of his mind. Talk to several Jesuits, strangers all of them, and their suavity and tone and gesture seem identical.[15] This is the reason why Mr Luxmoore, Hopkins's Highgate friend, gravely misunderstood the Society of Jesus and regretted Gerard's joining it. 'To go on with the Jesuits,' Mr Luxmoore wrote to Arthur Hopkins, 'you must become on many grave points a machine, without will, without conscience, & that to his nature was an impossibility.'[16] But this apparent blunting of the Jesuits' individualities inevitably redoubles their capacity for unselfish work. All thoughts, all passions, all delights, all that stir this mortal frame, all are seemingly beaten together, fused to one huge concentration of will that learns, obeys, directs, commands, organizes, by turns or all at once, and always triumphantly. The Jesuit is a pastor today, a professor tomorrow, an engineer the next day, an electioneering strategist the day after, an eager lexicographer or archaeologist or editor any day—but he is a Jesuit still, and no drifter, and no sham. The word of his Superior is the voice of God—and why not? 'The command expresses for the time being the will of God, as nearly as it can be ascertained.'[17] And, in this sense, the Jesuit discipline must surely bring a member of the Order, as Newman said it should, to God. The fact cannot be disputed: an army

[15] The impression of uniformity produced by the training need not be exaggerated. Though all Jesuits pass through the same mould, it has been remarked that the individuality of each is safeguarded and remains distinctive.
[16] *Letters*, III, p. 249.   [17] *Note-Books*, p. 447.

that is international, an Order that is several centuries old, whose disciplined units are a marvel, the Society of Jesus has been to non-Catholics at once enigmatic and ubiquitous, but anyhow deserving of unqualified admiration. But had Gerard Manley Hopkins any relevant place in this huge organization? Could it harbour a poet, to whom his trembling personality is of peculiar and perennial interest? Did Hopkins bury the poet—and could he really!—to become the soldier? Or was—monstrous thought—Hopkins not a poet at all?

It may be pointed out here, taking our cue from Sir Arthur Quiller-Couch, that though poetry is certainly a personal affair, the very greatest poetry is seraphically free from the taint of personality. How much of the respective poets do we encounter in *Ramayana, The Iliad, The Divine Comedy, The Book of Job,* and yet are not they all, in their own right, imperishable poetry? When a personal emotion, by whatever process of de-personalization, acquires a potent universality, and finds expression in terms of poetry, then is it, not merely pure poetry, but great poetry. Personal feelings and predilections are intuitively transported into the universal, and a trick of arranging words becomes a marvel in the realm of sheer language, not restrictively English or Tamil or Greek. It becomes a symbol of the eternal and the perfect before which criticism is dumb and all annotation a sacrilege. The process is not what is vulgarly called 'generalization'; it is something more and something vastly different. The de-personalization is not the substitution of a generalized dummy in the place of a vitally alive individual emotion; on the other hand, the emotion itself, by a single act of imaginative enlargement, is made to comprehend all humanity painfully struggling towards perfection. Faith need not cramp a poet's

THE LURE OF LOYOLA

imaginative facility; the soldier, the active medical practitioner, the missionary, they are none of them the contradictories of the poet. In fact, the sublimation of the mere self—earth-bound to a fault—into a universality that implicates the lives of every one of us should rather be a source of tremendous strength to the poet; it must give him the Sophoclean vision to see life steadily and to see it whole. In Mr Watkin's words—

'Thus in the fullness of aesthetic vision, at the point where art touches religion, tragedy gives place to a Divine Comedy, and suffering issues in a peace and joy which transmute it. Art is a transformation of the real in the light of the ideal, of nature in the light of spirit.... The artist also spreads out his hands to embrace the whole of nature, sub-human and human, in a generous and universal acceptance and love, then raises hands and eyes in aspiration to that higher World of Spirit whence its patterns derive.'[18]

Hopkins was indeed a genuine poet, and when he decided to burn most of what he had already written and to write no more, he honestly thought that only by giving up his 'all' could he hope to deserve the name of companion of Jesus; but, when years later, after he had completed his noviciate and established himself as a devout Catholic and earnest Jesuit, he began writing poetry, it was in a new voice altogether, distinctive in tone and timbre even to the point of occasional incomprehensibility, but undeniably the authentic voice of a human being. As Mrs Phare aptly puts it—

'While he was undergoing the arduous process of becoming a Jesuit, while his personality was having a character imposed upon it, he was not at one with himself and his poetry in consequence bore marks of a mind which,

[18] *A Philosophy of Form*, pp. 348-9.

if not sick, was in some way flawed: not whole and not mature. But when use and custom and perhaps grace had combined to make character and personality coincide, the useless, unfruitful conflict which spoilt his earlier poems disappeared.'[19]

The discipline of Loyola gave Hopkins's poetry a concentration, a compression in the use of language.[20] Jesuits, it has been observed, are men of deeds, not of empty words; and Hopkins's best poems became, as far as that could be accomplished, thoughts and words and deeds in one. It would be impossible in such poems to dissociate the words from the idea, or the experience from the poem. The Jesuit, indeed, did not kill the poet; one merely merged in the other. The sum was at last definitely greater than the component parts.

[19] E. E. Phare, *The Poetry of Gerard Manley Hopkins*, p. 18.
[20] cf. 'The Order, if it severely limited the range of his poetry, profoundly intensified it. In this intensification the Spiritual Exercises, acting upon a nature so tensely poised in itself between the sensuous and ideal, played a principal part.' (*The Times Literary Supplement*, 26 September 1942.)

VII. PROBATION

HOPKINS spent two years at the Roehampton noviciate. He continued to jot down in the Journals he maintained from 19 July 1868 onward whatever struck him as important in his surroundings. He kept two Journals, one descriptive and intellectual and the other spiritual; only the former has been published by Mr House, the spiritual Journal having been destroyed, probably by Hopkins himself. The Journal as we have it is largely a weather report from day to day; but there are also any number of Nature descriptions, revealing Hopkins's remarkable powers of observation and his insight into Nature's obscure processes and purposes. With the commencement of the Long Retreat on 16 September 1868, the entries in the Journal grow thinner, but never fail to be incisive and arresting. A few entries belonging to the Roehampton period might be given:

'A weeping-willow here is all green. The elms have long been in red bloom and yesterday (the 11th) I saw small leaves on the brushwood at their roots. Some primroses out. But a penance which I was doing from January 25 to July 25 prevented my seeing much that half-year.'[1]

'Yesterday morning I was dreaming I was with George Simcox and was considering how to get away in time to bring the bells here which as porter I had to ring (I was made porter on the 12th of the month, I think, and had the office for a little more than two months). I knew that I was dreaming and made this odd dilemma in my dream: either I am not really with Simcox and then it does not matter what I do, or if I am, waking will carry me off

[1] *Note-Books*, p. 121.

without my needing to do anything—and with this I was satisfied.'²

'... before I had always taken the sunset and the sun as quite out of gauge with each other, as indeed physically they are, for the eye after looking at the sun is blunted to everything else and if you look at the rest of the sunset you must cover the sun, but today I inscaped them together and made the sun the true eye and ace of the whole, as it is. It was all active and tossing out light and started as strongly forward from the field as a long stone or a boss in the knob of the chalice-stem: it is indeed by stalling it so that it falls into scape with the sky.'³

And so on, illustrations of inscape and instress, permutations and combinations of colour, judgements on the day's weather, dreams and comments on the psychology of dreams, and odd ghost stories, follow in an endless profusion, revealing everywhere the personality of the writer, if not directly, at least by necessary implication. Hopkins was a man for whom (in Professor Abbott's words) 'the visible world triumphantly exists, whose delight in colour is that of a painter'.⁴ Here is a notable extract from the Journal: 'When you climbed to the top of the tree and came out the sky looked as if you could touch it and it was as if you were in a world made up of these three colours, the green of the leaves lit through by the sun, the blue of the sky, and the grey blaze of their upper sides against it.'⁵ A man who could feel like that and write like that in spite of the discipline at the noviciate could never, never be lost to the realm of letters.

From Roehampton Hopkins proceeded to Stonyhurst in 1870. There, at St Mary's Hall, the house of studies for

---

² *Note-Books*, p. 126.   ³ ibid., p.129.
⁴ *Letters*, III, Introduction, p. xix.
⁵ *Note-Books*, p. 124.

Jesuit scholastics, Hopkins remained for three years. He gave an account of his life there in a letter to Baillie:

'I am going through a hard course of scholastic logic... which takes all the fair part of the day and leaves one fagged at the end for what remains. This makes the life painful to nature. I find now too late *how* to read—at least some books, *e.g.*, the classics: now I see things, now what I read tells, but I am obliged to read by snatches... this life here though it is hard is God's will for me as I most intimately know, which is more than violets knee-deep.'[6]

A year and a half later, Hopkins again wrote to Baillie: 'I am here for another year and now they are having at me with ethics and mechanics. Today is a whole holiday: I spent a miserable morning over formulas for the lever....'[7] While he was thus most of the time bending his inclinations in the direction of dry, intellectual inquiries and studies, Hopkins, the creature of emotion and of memory, fully aware of the cross-currents in life and Nature, was at the same time expressing himself in the Journal and Letters. In a letter to his sister, Kate Hopkins, he refers to his vaccination, but presently his tender sensibility reveals itself:

'As I came down one of the galleries from the room I saw one of our young men standing there looking at a picture. I wondered why he stayed by himself and did not join the rest and then afterwards I remembered that he had had the small-pox and was deeply marked with it and all his good looks gone which he would have had and he did not want to face the others at that time when they were having their fun taking safe precautions against catching what it was too late for him to take any precautions against.'[8]

[6] *Letters*, III, pp. 87-8.   [7] ibid., p. 91.
[8] ibid., p. 42.

There is also an entry in the Journal which beautifully brings out not only Hopkins's humanitarianism but also his profound humility:

'Dec. 17-18 (1871) at night—Rescued a little kitten that was perched in the sill of the round window at the sink over the gasjet and dared not jump down. I heard her mew a piteous long time till I could bear it no longer; but I make a note of it because of her gratitude after I had taken her down, which made her follow me about and at each turn of the stairs as I went down leading her to the kitchen run back a few steps up and try to get up to lick me through the banisters from the flight above.'[9]

The miscellaneous entries in the Journal, of course, are as interesting as ever; there are several brief jottings which constitute a sort of diary of the Franco-Prussian War; there are skeleton accounts of various minor trips; there are notes, exultingly jotted down, expressing the unsullied joy of discovering some new inscape or other; there are occasional references to illness, to deaths or marriages of relations or friends, to the 'deathwatch ticking' in a room in the Old Magazine at the College; there are, more occasionally, references to confessions, masses, and other religious observances; and there are sketches in pencil and descriptions that not unsuccessfully capture and hold before our eyes the fleeting impressions of enraptured moments:

'It was a glowing yellow sunset. Pendle and all the hill rinsed clear, their heights drawn with a brimming light, in which windows or anything that could catch fluttered and laughed with the blaze—all bounded by the taught outline of a mealy blue shadow covering the valley, which was moist and giving up mist. . . .'[10]

'The Horned Violet is a pretty thing, gracefully lashed. Even in withering the flower ran through beautiful inscapes

---

[9] *Note-Books*, p. 156.   [10] ibid., p. 147.

by the screwing up of the petals into straight little barrels or tubes. . . .'¹¹

'It is pretty to see the dance and swagging of the light green tongues or ripples of waves in a place locked between rocks.'¹²

It is impossible to withhold admiration from so painstaking and contrapuntal an adoration of Nature's myriad hues and many-toned significances. The sensuous man in Hopkins, so diligently and willingly repressed at other times, asserted himself exquisitely in these miniature prose-poems on Nature's infinite variety. It is when we read such notes in the Journal and 'inscape' them with Hopkins's other writings—letters and poems and even sermons—that we feel the full truth of Professor Abbott's statement:

'Gerard Hopkins is, indeed, all of a piece. Whether poem or letter or sermon one feels that the whole of him, the full weight of his character, the essence of the man at that moment, is behind the writing. . . . They bear the imprint of the same rare mind and spirit, they have the same disciplined honesty and intensity of conviction.'¹³

Hopkins returned to Roehampton in September 1873 and acted as Professor of Rhetoric for some time. Restless introspection within a repressed circle of experience is still the trouble with Hopkins, and one is not surprised to find him lying in bed one night and furiously contemplating on the ugliness of his name 'till I was so mortified that even now it is a cure to vainglory to recall the thought'.¹⁴ This time Hopkins is a professor, not a novice; hence he is enjoying more freedom apparently; at any rate, there are occasional references in the letters to literature, journalism,

---

¹¹ *Note-Books*, p. 149.   ¹² ibid., p. 165.
¹³ *Letters*, III, Introduction, p. xx.
¹⁴ ibid., p. 44.

even to politics. Hopkins visits the National Gallery, goes to hear the Lord Chief Justice summing up in the Titchbourne case, gazes appreciatively at beautiful Japanese work in the Kensington museum, takes Brother Tournade to see and gather bluebells, visits the Academy and makes profuse notes on what he has as usual acutely observed, pays a visit to the Oratory, and manages to hear some speeches during the sitting of the Lords, and later of the Commons also: it is all so delightfully, insinuatingly described in the Journals and Letters.

During his Professorship of Rhetoric, Hopkins made many important notes on the subject, and these have now been printed by Mr House in the *Note-Books*. ' "Rhetoric" in Jesuit schools and colleges is used generally, as "Classics" in others, to cover literary subjects based on Latin and Greek.'[15] These notes that Hopkins thought necessary to jot down relate to 'Rhythm and the other structural parts of Rhetoric', and there is also an illuminating note on 'Poetry and Verse'. In these notes Hopkins was fumbling to express certain original ideas of his own regarding the mechanism of verse, though he was able to reduce them to a regular system only later on in his Preface to his manuscript poems.

In September 1874 Hopkins was translated to St Beuno's College, St Asaph, North Wales, to study theology. Three years afterwards, Hopkins was still at St Asaph, and wrote to Baillie: 'I am preparing for my last examination in moral theology. You see moral theology covers the whole of life and to know it it is best to begin by knowing everything, as medicine, law, history, banking. . . I hope to be ordained priest next September and after that shall be here,

---

[15] *Note-Books*, Introduction, p. xxviii.

I suppose, for another twelvemonth.'[16] For the rest, Hopkins had around him the abundance of Nature, and this furnished him with matter for ever so many more notes on birds, clouds, thunderstorms, and mountains. Again and again, one collides against the most unusual descriptions, puzzling correlations of 'instress' and 'inscape':

'It was a leaden sky, braided or roped with cloud, and the earth in dead colours, grave but distinct. The heights by Snowdon were hidden by the clouds but not from distance or dimness. The nearer hills, the other side of the valley, shewed a hard and beautifully detached and glimmering brim against the light, which was lifting there. All the length of the valley the skyline of the hills was flowingly written all along upon the sky. A blue bloom, a sort of meal, seemed to have spread upon the distant south, enclosed by a basin of hills. Looking all round but most in looking far up the valley I felt the instress and charm of Wales.'[17]

'We went up to the castle but not in: standing before the gateway I had an instress which only the true old work gives from the strong and noble inscape of the pointed arch.'[18]

Here and there Hopkins's frequent use of 'scape' and 'stress' reads like an irritating jargon. But in passages like the above—and their name is, of course, legion—the poetic vision that sees the universe as ordered motion and the religious faith that inscapes a cosmos underlying the apparent chaos are in profound and beautiful harmony.[19] Hopkins

---

[16] *Letter*s, III, p. 95.   [17] *Note-Books*, p. 210.
[18] ibid., pp. 216-17.
[19] cf. Pick, pp. 32, 35, 36: 'This association of the experience of beauty with a religious experience becomes increasingly more and more central for Hopkins.... In many of his later poems this sacramental view of nature is developed; in it the poet and the priest reach through the things of the sense to hidden beauties.... While many of the mystics have closed their eyes the better to concentrate on the things of the spirit.... Hopkins opened them wide to find the one ablaze in the many.'

could have affirmed, as the Sufi mystic Ni'matu'llah of Kisman did, 'Mirrors a hundred thousand I see, but the face of that Giver of Life is One'.[20]

[20] Translation by E. G. Browne.

VIII. 'THE WRECK OF THE DEUTSCHLAND'

FOR seven years after entering the Jesuit noviciate at Roehampton Hopkins did not write, according to his own admission, any poems except 'two or three little presentation pieces which occasion called for'.[1] Two of these latter are supposed to be 'Rosa Mystica' and 'Ad Mariam'. Neither can be classed with Hopkins's best or characteristic poetry. No doubt, they are important from a purely religious point of view; and no doubt therefore they will appeal to Catholics much more than to others. In 'Rosa Mystica' Hopkins attempts a symbolical interpretation of the Rose, its beauty and its mystery. The following is a typical stanza—

> Is Mary that Rose, then? Mary, the Tree?
> But the Blossom, the Blossom there, who can it be?
> Who can her Rose be? It could be but One:
> Christ Jesus, our Lord—her God and her Son.
>   In the Gardens of God, in the daylight divine
>   Shew me thy Son, Mother, Mother of mine.[2]

The last two lines are a refrain, and must produce its proper effect when recited in chorus. 'Ad Mariam', again, judged as poetry, is unsatisfactory. It intrigued Bridges: 'This is in five stanzas of eight lines, in direct and competent imitation of Swinburne . . . and, unless Fr Hopkins's views of poetic form had been provisionally deranged or suspended, the verses can hardly be attributed to him without some impeachment of his sincerity; and that being altogether above suspicion, I would not yield to the rather strong presumption which their technical skill supplies in

[1] *Letters*, II, p. 14.   [2] *Poems*, No. 85.

favour of his authorship.'³ The Swinburnian lilt of the poem can be seen in lines like—

> With eyes that smile through the tears of the hours,
> With joy for to-day and hope for to-morrow
>   And the promise of Summer within her breast . . . .
>
> The praise of the lips and the hearts of us bring to thee
>   Thee, oh maiden, most worthy of praise . . . .

Even otherwise, the poem, with its neatness of diction and the religious urgency of its theme, must have pleased the audience for which it had originally been intended. A responsive chord must have been struck in the hearts of the devout by the note of—

> O thou, proud mother and much proud maiden—
>   Maid yet mother as May hath been—
> To thee we tender the beauties all
> Of the month by men called virginal.⁴

However, these presentation pieces do not belong, on Hopkins's own admission, to his serious Muse. The same Hopkins could later, in poems like 'The May Magnificat' and 'The Blessed Virgin compared to the Air We Breathe', transfigure the Marian theme into things of enchanting and enduring beauty.

Hopkins, then, had not written poetry as such, serious poetry, for a period of seven years. But, as he later explained to his friend Canon Dixon, 'when in the winter of '75 the *Deutschland* was wrecked in the mouth of the Thames and five Franciscan nuns, exiles from Germany by the Falk Laws, aboard of her were drowned I was affected by the account and happening to say so to my rector he said that he wished someone would write a poem on the subject. On this hint I set to work and, though my hand was out

---

³ *Poems*, p. 102.   ⁴ ibid., No. 84.

at first, produced one. I had long had haunting my ear the echo of a new rhythm which now I realized on paper.'[5] The poem referred to here is 'The Wreck of the *Deutschland*', in thirty-five stanzas and divided into two parts. 'The poem stands,' says Bridges, 'logically as well as chronologically in the front of his book, like a great dragon folded in the gate to forbid all entrance, and confident in his strength from past success.'[6] Difficult, undoubtedly, the poem is; amazing, tantalizing, obscure in many places; and yet, it is a substantial poem and a supremely moving poem. For seven years, from the age of twenty-four to thirty-two, Hopkins had with violence tried to divorce himself from poetry; he had spent them in austerities, in a discipline of the faculties of mind and body. But Hopkins had never ceased to be a poetic person; and when circumstances enabled him to lift the self-imposed ban on the writing of poetry, the so long bottled-up energy burst through its bonds and welled up in an excruciating jet of melody. Complicated, certainly, the melody is to ears rather attuned to the simpler notes of Tennyson or Byron: but it is unmistakably a melody and not a cacophony, a melody that is complex, self-controlled, and animated by the rushing tumult of its underlying passion. Professor Abbott correctly points out that 'behind the momentous "Wreck of the *Deutschland*" . . . lie the meditation, experience, and priestly training of more than seven years'.[7]

This is the first stanza—
> Thou mastering me
> God! giver of breath and bread;
> World's strand, sway of the sea;
> Lord of living and dead;

[5] *Letters*, II, p. 14.   [6] *Poems*, p. 104.
[7] *Letters*, I, Introduction, p. xxvi.

> Thou hast bound bones and veins in me,
> fastened me flesh,
> And after it almost unmade, what with dread,
> Thy doing: and dost thou touch me afresh?
> Over again I feel thy finger and find thee.[8]

Like the Choruses in Swinburne's *Atalanta in Calydon*, but in a different and more profound and manly way, these lines make a disturbingly vital use of assonance and alliteration and of a seemingly deceptive rhythm. While Swinburne produces in his most characteristic verse a temporary lulling of the senses through the opiate of constant alliteration and the dizzy motion of the galloping anapaests, Hopkins pursues a far subtler strategy that necessarily keeps our faculties alert. The thirty-five stanzas, broken up into two parts of ten and twenty-five stanzas respectively, have but two affirmations of faith and one illustrative experience, but these are artfully soldered into one admirable poetic entity by the unity of Hopkins's vision.[9] God is 'giver of breath and bread'; He is preserver and Destroyer in one. What is His attitude towards His creatures? Rebel man—'frail clay, nay but foul clay'—must be mastered and chastened by God; frail, foul clay must be beaten hard, smelted in the forge of suffering, till it is purified and transmuted into precious gold. Five Franciscan nuns are drowned—that, too, is God's doing: it is ocular proof that God's manifestations, however strange and however fearful, are inescapable, and are,

---

[8] *Poems*, No. 4. For a detailed illuminating analysis of 'The Wreck of the *Deutschland*', I must refer the reader to the third chapter of Pick's book.

[9] cf. Pick, p. 41: '. . . its meaning is Christ: it is the story of the Passion and Redemption working themselves out in the lives of men. . . The poem narrates the story of a nun and of a poet, Gerard Manley Hopkins, who read in the temporal events surrounding them an eternal message from their God.'

in the final analysis, just—and not only just, but born of an abounding abiding love. Man rebels, is mastered, and finds grace; the nuns are drowned, but they wake up heroic and victorious in the sinless spaces of Heaven. There is stress and storm, and there are sombre significances—but God is behind them all, and is the Ordainer of the final order that emerges from all this tumult and rush and apparent waste.

These ideas which constitute the emotional core of the poem can be apprehended by one and all; but superimposed on these are also certain Christian dogmas, especially those relating to the Incarnation and Redemption: these can be explained in the words of Mr Bernard Kelly:

'The Incarnation and Redemption, which have gladdened the destiny of man, have also profoundly affected his relation to the beauty of this world. For if the world is news of God it is also news from an Incarnate God. . . . Beauty is signed with the Cross, and is an invitation to the Cross. And this is not an intellectual or devotional construction put on the world by the faithful, but is of the very nature of the world and of beauty, for the world is news of God.'[10]

He subsists in all things, all creatures, all activities; He is subject and object both. And it is not difficult for a true lover of poetry to believe in these ideas, for the time being at any rate, so that he can seize in an act of attention the full significance of 'The Wreck of the *Deutschland*'.

One of the pivotal stanzas in the poem is the last but one in Part the First—

> Be adored among men,
> God, three-numberèd form;
> Wring thy rebel, dogged in den,
> Man's malice, with wrecking and storm.

---

[10] *The Mind and Poetry of Gerard Manley Hopkins*, S.J. (Pepler and Sewell, St Dominic's Press, Ditchling, 1935).

> Beyond saying sweet, past telling of tongue,
> Thou art lightning and love, I found it, a winter
> and warm;
> Father and fondler of heart thou hast wrung:
> Hast thy dark descending and most art merciful then.[11]

God's ways are mysterious; His dealings with men may not always be explained in human categories; He is illimitable, He contains multitudes. Man may err and rebel, but he could be subdued, and he could be redeemed through suffering and grace—

> With an anvil-ding
> And with fire in him forge thy will
> Or rather, rather then, stealing as Spring
> Through him, melt him but master him still.

Since the Incarnation—since Christ's taking a human habitation and name—the world has been charged with the glory of God—and the vestiges of God, had we eyes to see, are everywhere visible. There is but one truth, then— a supreme, fearful, splendorous truth: '*Ipse* the only one, Christ, King, Head.' To apprehend and *be* this truth must therefore be the summit of Christian aspiration.

Part the Second deals with the nuns, their earthly travail and their final spiritual triumph in heaven. The intimations of brute Nature, of adorable tranquillity, of doubt and despair, of illumination and triumph, are thrown together

---

[11] cf. Sri Aurobindo:
> The God of Wrath, the God of Love are one,
> Not least He loves when most He smites. Alone
> Who rises above fear and plays with grief,
> Defeat and death, inherits full relief
> From blindness and beholds the single Form,
> Love masking Terror, Peace supporting storm.
> The Friend of Man helps him with Life and Death,
> Until he knows.

(*Collected Poems and Plays*, Vol. II, p. 129.)

with their overtones and undertones, till at last the whole situation, terrible in its pathos, comes to one in a flash. The stanzas roll precipitately forward, in jerks and jumps and headlong falls; and the diction, full of fresh significances, is instinct with a proper harmony. In the evocation of a heart-rending moment, in the translation of death-shrieks, in the assertion of a Faith that countenances no defeat, in picturing desolation or symbolizing undying hope, Hopkins's verse is equal to every occasion. The descriptive passages contain faint echoes of various contemporaries of Hopkins—but nevertheless they are vitally his own. The evocation of the storm is masterly—

> ....and so the sky keeps,
>   For the infinite air is unkind,
> And the sea flint-flake, black-backed in the regular blow,
>   Sitting Eastnortheast, in cursed quarter, the wind;
>   Wiry and white-fiery and whirlwind-swivellèd snow
> Spins to the widow-making unchilding unfathering deeps.
>
>   She drove in the dark to leeward,
>   She struck—not a reef or a rock
> But the combs of a smother of sand: night drew her
>   Dead to the Kentish Knock;
> And she beat the bank down with her bows and the ride
>   of her keel:
> The breakers rolled on her beam with ruinous shock;
>   And canvas and compass, the whorl and the wheel
> Idle for ever to waft her or wind her with, these
>   she endured.[12]

The ship is sinking; the passengers are wild, distraught; hope though hopeless still flutters amidst despair; the roar of the waves and the lashing fury of the wind mix with the

---

[12] In many respects 'The Wreck of the *Deutschland*' and Tagore's 'The Sea-waves' deserve to be studied comparatively.

piercing cries of the passengers, the hurrying and impotent scurrying. It is all made vivid with superb art; the very phrases, and their articulateness through the agitated urgency of the rhythm, re-create the tragedy of the shipwreck; and they also underline the fact that all, the pain and the despair as well as the courage and the ecstasy, are a fulfilment of God. There is now an ominous calm; and the terrible prospect is, as it were, 'humped in silence': but indeed, it is the silence that is a prelude to spiritual illumination, to the thrill of approaching beatitude—

> Ah, touched in your bower of bone
> Are you! turned for an exquisite smart,
> Have you! make words break from me here all alone,
> Do you!—mother of being in me, heart.

Then follow the moving stanzas about the nun—'calling a master, her master and mine!' She would bring hope to them all, to the wailing tumult shuddering at the prospect; she would rear herself 'to divine ears'. And yet she comes from the same Germany, the Germany that has neither grace nor charity—

> O Deutschland, double a desperate name!
> O world wide of its good!
> But Gertrude, lily, and Luther, are two of a town,
> Christ's lily and beast of the waste wood:
> From life's dawn it is drawn down,
> Abel is Cain's brother and breasts they have
>   sucked the same.

The Germany that produced a Goethe is also the Germany that produced in our time an Adolf Hitler: and Ernst Toller and Dr Goebbels were Germans both!

The nun braves the storm, dares it, accepts it: she
screams loudly, drowning the wailing and the raging—

> .... 'O Christ, Christ, come quickly':
> The Cross to her she calls Christ to her, christens
> her wild-worst Best.

There is a suggestion, in a later stanza, of the mystery of the
Immaculate Conception—

> Feast of the one woman without stain.
> For so conceivèd, so to conceive thee is done;
> But here was heart-throe, birth of a brain,
> Word, that heard and kept thee and uttered thee
> outright.

Other notes are also distinctly heard. There is stark despair
itself in—

> .... What could he do
> With the burl of the fountains of air, buck and
> the flood of the wave?

There is verbal camouflage of puzzlement in—

> Why, tears! is it? tears; such a melting, a
> madrigal start!
> Never-eldering revel and river of youth,
> What can it be, this glee? the good you have there
> of your own?

And, finally, there is a quiet and unflinching assertion of
faith in—

> .... past all
> Grasp God, throned behind
> Death with a sovereignty that heeds but hides,
> bodes but abides.

Read at a stretch, and in a responsive frame of mind, 'The Wreck of the *Deutschland*' does seem to be, with its cross-currents and emotional eddies, a harmony that co-exists with and at the same time triumphs over various disharmonies. In a Platonic dialogue entitled 'On the Origin of Beauty',[13] Hopkins elaborates the idea that all beauty is merely the manifestation of the principle of agreement in disagreement: in poetry, for instance, artifices like rhyme, alliteration, assonance, regular rhythm itself, all contribute towards the same end; so do figures of speech like metaphor, simile, antithesis and contrast. In 'The Wreck of the *Deutschland*', not only the technique, but the very theme itself, is a demonstration of agreement in disagreement, having both unity and subordination. The outer 'form' or 'design' of a thing, its formal beauty, holds together the shapeless protoplasms that compose and constitute its matter, and gives them this 'agreement in disagreement' on the purely physical plane. The 'rhythm' of a poem, of life itself, holds together the fluid, vapoury ebullitions and storms of life, and gives them an ordered movement, a purposive existence; and this is also a manifestation of agreement in disagreement, of unity and subordination, but on the emotional plane, the human plane. Finally, the 'inner form' or the utter truth of a phenomenon, of the pageant of life itself, of the world-stress that has us in its grip, is also a similar principle with a similar *modus operandi*: it holds together the ethical questions and heart-searchings thrown up by the pattern and the rhythm of the mysterious universe; it is a synoptic vision that locates the underlying norm of spiritual harmony; its purifying efficacy enables one to be at home in the midst of the spiritual cross-currents set up in life, and helps one, too, to acquire and to preserve the faith

[13] *Note-Books*, pp. 54-91.

that the ways of God, however intriguing, are just, inherently and finally and all along. Such a perception is surely profounder, and spiritually more consoling, than the emotion that sustains the great poetic tragedies in world literature. For, to quote Mr Edward Watkin once more, 'the dramatist tells of the tragedy arising from the conflict between good and evil, form and disorder, as seen in its process by a vision too shortsighted to behold the end. For the ultimate vision of religious faith resolves tragedy in triumph, and leaves only the epic of achievement and the lyric of praise. The story of the Cross, for all its suffering and defeat, is no longer a tragedy when the Resurrection is known to be its sequel.'[14] So interpreted, the tragedy of the five Franciscan nuns is no tragedy at all, no defeat at the hands of Death, Desire and Incapacity, but a divine fulfilment, ensuring their greater glory in the hereafter.

The charge of obscurity has been levelled against 'The Wreck' times without number. Bridges read the poem once, failed to 'understand' it, and kept it aside: Hopkins, on being told of it, gently remonstrated with his friend:

'I must tell you I am sorry that you never read the Deutschland again. Granted that it needs study and is obscure, for indeed I was not over-desirous that the meaning of all should be quite clear, at least unmistakable, you might, without the effort that to make it all out would seem to have required, have nevertheless read it so that lines and stanzas should be left in the memory and superficial impressions deepened, and have liked some without exhausting all.... When a new thing, such as my ventures in the Deutschland are, is presented us our first criticisms are not our truest, best, most homefelt, or most lasting but what comes easiest on the instant.... The Deutschland on her first run worked very much and unsettled you, thickening

[14] *A Philosophy of Form*, p. 346.

and clouding your mind with vulgar mudbottom and common sewage....'[15]

Again: 'Obscurity I do and will try to avoid so far as is consistent with excellences higher than clearness at a first reading.'[16] This puts the matter squarely. Hopkins is obscure, more or less as Browning is obscure, because there is compression carried almost to breaking point, and not, as sometimes Shelley or Swinburne is obscure, because there is no thought to comprehend, no logical sequence to follow. His poetry, like the Sanskrit poetry of Venkatanātha, is to be described as *narikēlapāka*; the outer shell should be broken before the kernel can be tasted, but the kernel is certainly there. Hopkins's obscurity, says Mr John Sparrow, a critic who is not at all enthusiastic about 'modernist' poetry, 'is usually due to ellipses, unusual word-order, use of strange words, or description of one kind of sensation (in the manner of Miss Sitwell) in terms of another'.[17] Here, for instance, with the barest minimum of words, the Incarnation is described—

> It dates from day
> Of his going in Galilee;
> Warm-laid grave of a womb-life grey;
> Manger, maiden's knee;
> The dense and the driven Passion, and frightful sweat.[18]

The compression and allusiveness of such poetry no doubt demand from the reader both earnestness and concentration; but there *are* readers who are quite prepared for this discipline and are very willing indeed to spend whole hours reading such 'obscure' poetry half-aloud, revelling in its

---

[15] *Letters*, I, pp. 50-51.   [16] ibid., p. 54.
[17] *Sense and Poetry* (Constable, 1934), footnote on p. xx.
[18] *Poems*, No. 4. st. 7.

imagery, its rhythm, and its spiritual potency. Only prejudice and short-sightedness will define 'poetry' too narrowly and refuse the title to such a masterpiece as 'The Wreck of the *Deutschland*'.

IX. A ROLLING STONE

HOPKINS had found his true voice at last, and what to many would appear an incredible concoction, the Jesuit-poet, had aggressively come into being. No doubt the Jesuit paper, *The Month*, did not dare to publish the poem—its singularities were too many! But it did not matter. The poet Hopkins had the intellectual companionship of other poets, Robert Bridges and Canon Dixon, and later of Coventry Patmore; the poems were to pass to and fro in manuscript, with queries, suggestions, explanations, corrections, criticisms and appreciations. Hopkins persevered; he was not sure that his poems would ever be published, he felt rather the contrary; and yet he could not help, now and then, realizing his emotions and experiences in terms of poetry. That circumstances might never favour the actual publication of his poems was a melancholy thought: it recurs in several letters to his friends, especially to Canon Dixon who was very eager that Hopkins should publish his poems. 'Even the impulse to writing is wanting, for I have no thought of publishing',[1] he wrote to Dixon in 1878, after the '*Deutschland*' and several other poems had already been written. Next year again he wrote to Dixon:

'(1) I have no thought of publishing until all circumstances favour, which I do not know that they ever will, and it seems that one of them should be that the suggestion to publish should come from one of our own people; (2) to allow such a notice[2] would be on my part a sort of insubordination to or doubledealing with my superiors. But

---
[1] *Letters*, II, p. 15.
[2] Dixon had offered to give an 'abrupt footnote', in his forthcoming book, on Hopkins and his poetry.

nevertheless I sincerely thank you for your kind willingness to do me a service. The life I lead is liable to many mortifications but the want of fame as a poet is the least of them. I could wish, I allow, that my pieces could at some time become known but in some spontaneous way, so to speak, and without my forcing.'[3]

But Canon Dixon continued to ply Father Hopkins with embarrassing appeals. 'The more I study your work', he wrote, 'the more I admire it: and the more I regret the fate by which, as Bridges says, it still "unfortunately remains in manuscript", and seems doomed to linger there.'[4] But Hopkins would not be persuaded, though it is unlikely that the determination to 'sacrifice' present fame as a poet was arrived at without any struggle. He described that the Jesuit ideal is of a man 'who in the world is as dead to the world as if he were buried in the cloister';[5] this ideal is so high

'that a higher can be found nowhere else. The question then for me is not whether I am willing (if I may guess what is in your mind) to make a sacrifice of hopes of fame (let us suppose), but whether I am not to undergo a severe judgement from God for the lothness I have shown in making it, for the reserves I may have in my heart made, for the backward glances I have given with my hand upon the plough, for the waste of time the very compositions you admire may have caused and their preoccupation of the mind which belonged to more sacred or more binding duties, for the disquiet and the thoughts of vainglory they have given rise to. A purpose may look smooth and perfect from

[3] *Letters*, II, p. 28.   [4] ibid., p. 51.
[5] ibid., p. 76.   cf. Herbert Read : 'It is easy to regret that Hopkins's conscience would not allow him to spend time on poetry, but we must remember that the poet was the man— that his poetic make was complementary to his religious make, and that to ask for a different man is to ask for a different poet.' (*A Coat of Many Colours*, 1945, p. 162.)

without but be frayed and faltering from within. I have never wavered in my vocation, but I have not lived up to it ... I can scarcely fancy myself asking a superior to publish a volume of my verses and I own that humanly there is very little likelihood of that ever coming to pass.... But there is more peace and it is the holier lot to be unknown than to be known.'[6]

Hopkins has here revealed the whole of himself—his chastity of mind, his humility, his tenderness, his sensitiveness, his regrets, his final resignation.

But while the cheerless thought that his poems will for long, probably ever, remain in manuscript may have deterred him from writing much or writing frequently, there were also two consoling considerations. Hopkins himself had written, in his very first letter to Dixon, expressing regret that the Canon's poetry was so little known; and he had received the characteristic reply: 'When I read your letter, and whenever I take it out of my pocket to look at it, I feel that I prefer to have been so known and prized by one, than to have had the ordinary appreciation of many.'[7] Hopkins too must have felt the same elation, the same soul's satisfaction, that choice spirits like Bridges and Dixon, themselves considerable poets, did prize his poems greatly, did indeed *love* them.[8] Hopkins, on his part, went further in his second letter to Dixon: 'Fame whether won or lost is a thing which lies in the award of a random, reckless, incompetent, and unjust judge, the public, the multitude. The only just judge, the only just literary critic, is Christ, who prizes, is proud of, and admires, more than any man, more than the receiver himself can, the gifts of his own making.'[9] Here Hopkins exhorts his correspondent to place his literary works before the justest and greatest tribunal

[6] *Letters*, II, pp. 88-9. [7] ibid., p. 4.
[8] *Letters*, III, p. 208. [9] *Letters*, II, p. 8.

possible, and abide by the verdict. Hopkins must have done the same, must have by and by learned to do the same; and hence the poems he wrote after the '*Deutschland*', off and on during the remaining twelve years of his life, were of a rich quality and were destined to exert no mean influence on his friends and on later generations of poets.

'The Wreck of the *Deutschland*' had been composed when Hopkins was still at St Beuno's College, Wales. In 1877 he was ordained priest after a probation of nine years. His Journal bears ample witness to his wanderings in North Wales amidst scenes that made him intoxicated with Nature's loveliness. But soon after his ordination Hopkins was made, first preacher at Farm Street Church, London, and later Sub-minister or Bursar at Mount St Mary's College, Chesterfield. 'Much against my inclination' Hopkins went to London,[10] and from the pulpit intrigued his audience by comparing the Catholic Church to a milch-cow, 'wandering in a beautiful meadow, chewing the green grass, and transforming it into ambrosial milk, the thirsty calves the while eagerly hanging by the udders'. It was this occasional singularity in presentation that frightened his superiors and made them ask him to 'write out each sermon before delivering it; but it must be confessed that poor Gerard seldom preached the same sermon he had faithfully prepared!'[11] At Mount St Mary's College, Chesterfield,

---

[10] *Letters*, I, p. 43. Dr Pick has attempted a detailed study of Hopkins's sermons at London and elsewhere in the fifth chapter of his book. His verdict is as follows: 'He (Hopkins) did not have more than mediocre success as a preacher, though his superiors tried hard to find a congenial place for him. . . . The sermons show a constant effort to appeal to his audience. There is great orderliness in all of them, a logical schematic development which makes lucid reading. But often the sermons suggest the class-room treatise or disputation.'

[11] Lahey, p. 133.

Hopkins had to do, among other things, house-keeping, preaching and accounting. Obviously he did not relish his work: 'Life here is as dank as ditch-water and has some of the other qualities of ditch-water: at least I know that I am reduced to great weakness by diarrhoea, which lasts too, as if I were poisoned.'[12] Bridges offered to go to Chesterfield to help Hopkins to recover: the latter's reply incidentally explains the origin of another of Hopkins's poems, 'The Loss of the *Eurydice*': 'I should have lost all shame if under any circumstances I had allowed such a thing to be as for you to come hundreds of miles to cure me.... My muse turned utterly sullen in the Sheffield smoke-ridden air and I had not written a line till the foundering of the Eurydice the other day and that worked on me and I am making a poem....'[13]

The next year found Hopkins at the Stonyhurst College, Blackburn, but not for long. Soon he moved to town, and wrote to Bridges, in a quiet note of resignation: 'I am, so far as I know, permanently here, but permanence with us is ginger-bread permanence; cobweb, soapsud, and frost-weather permanence.'[14] Under date 8 August 1878, Hopkins again wrote to Bridges: 'Next Sunday's sermon must be learnt better than last's. I was very little nervous at the beginning and not at all after. It was pure forgetting and flurry. The delivery was not good, but I hope to get a good one in time. I shall welcome any criticisms which are not controversy.'[15] Bridges had constituted one of the congregation, and hence this apologia.

Hopkins was soon on the move again. He spent the yearly retreat of eight days at Beaumont Lodge, Old Windsor, and then went to stay at St Aloysius' Church,

---

[12] *Letters*, I, p. 47.
[13] ibid., pp. 47-8.
[14] ibid., p. 55.
[15] ibid., p. 57.,

Oxford, for a period of ten months. When a further attempt at persuading Hopkins to publish his poetry was made, this time by Bridges, the answer was again a polite but very firm refusal to move of his own accord in the matter: 'All therefore that I think of doing is to keep my verses together in one place—at present I have not even correct copies—that, if anyone should like, they might be published after my death. And that again is unlikely, as well as remote.'[16] At Oxford, Hopkins was presumably happy; he certainly found the Oxford townspeople 'very deserving of affection —though somewhat stiff, stand-off, and depressed.'[17] Presently, there was another jerk of the kaleidoscope, and Hopkins was transferred to Liverpool as Preacher at the St Francis Xavier's Church. Between Oxford and Liverpool there was an interregnum which Hopkins spent at St Joseph's, Bedford Leigh, in Lancashire.

In Liverpool Hopkins's duties kept him very busy. With genial humour he wrote to Bridges, begging pardon for the delay in writing to him: 'The teapot of inclination has been tilted several times till the spout of intention very nearly teemed out the liquor of execution (I am speaking of myself now ... and must point out the extraordinary merit of the figure I am employing: I shall work it up), but till now it has not filled the cup and saucer of communication.'[18] From his letters we learn further that Hopkins was also engaged on a new style of music, 'something standing to ordinary music as sprung rhythm to common rhythm.'[19] But he was definitely run down in spirits. 'Every impulse and spring of art seems to have died in me, except for music, and that I pursue under almost an impossibility

---

[16] *Letters*, I, p. 66.
[17] *Letters*, III, p. 98.
[18] *Letters*, I, p. 100.
[19] ibid., p. 103.

of getting on.'[20] And elsewhere: 'I never could write; time and spirits were wanting; one is so fagged, so harried and gallied up and down.'[21] It was during this period, however, that he sent an amusing letter to Baillie, bifurcated and counter-pointed in parallel columns.[22]

From Liverpool Hopkins proceeded in August 1881 to St Joseph's, Glasgow, and spent there the interval between then and 10 October, when he was due at the Roehampton noviciate for the 'tertianship'. The second probation was to last for the next ten months, ending on St Ignatius' feast on 31 July 1882. In February 1882 Hopkins wrote to Bridges warning him that 'the right to read our letters claimed by the Society of its subjects but mostly not exercised is here a realized fact; so consult your own taste about what you will say and leave unsaid'.[23] It is no complaint that Hopkins is making here, but merely stating a fact: on the contrary, he seems to have enjoyed the supreme bounty of peace at Roehampton, for, he wrote to Dixon: 'My mind is here more at peace than it has ever been and I would gladly live all my life, if it were so to be, in as great or a greater seclusion from the world and be busied only with God. But in the midst of outward occupations not only the mind is drawn away from God, which may be at the call of duty and be God's will, but unhappily the will too is entangled, worldly interests freshen, and worldly ambitions revive.'[24]

In the meantime Hopkins was required to do some parish work in Preston and then to take part in a Mission to Maryport;[25] on his return journey, Hopkins contrived to meet Dixon at the Hayton Vicarage, Carlisle. Dixon was

[20] *Letters*, I, p. 124.
[22] *Letters*, III, pp. 100-101.
[24] *Letters*, II, pp. 75-6.
[21] ibid., p. 110.
[23] *Letters*, I, p. 141.
[25] *Letters*, I, p. 143.

shy; but Hopkins adds, 'I think that for myself I have very little shyness left in me, but I cannot communicate my own feeling to another.'[26] (Is this a generalization about all Jesuits?)

At the conclusion of the third year of the noviciate, Hopkins was appointed to teach at the Stonyhurst College, Blackburn. 'I am here', he wrote to Baillie later on, 'to coach classics for the London University Intermediate (say Moderations) and B.A. (say Greats) examinations. I like my pupils and do not wholly dislike the work, but I fall into or continue in a heavy weary state of body and mind in which my go is gone. . . . I make no way with what I read, and seem but half a man. It is a sad thing to say.' But, as usual, Canon Dixon consoled and encouraged him: 'My own experience is that any teaching, any literary work is good for the mind provided that it be literary, by which I include philosophy and exclude mathematics.'[27] Yet a note of weariness is perceptible here and there—weariness of body and of mind, though not of the soul. Hopkins could not certainly have relished, though he willingly enough acquiesced in, his being constantly moved about like a rolling stone. On 26 July 1883, Hopkins wrote to Bridges ever so gently bemoaning the precariousness of his appointments: 'It seems likely that I shall be removed; where I have no notion. But I have long been Fortune's football and am blowing up the bladder of resolution big and buxom for another kick of her foot. I shall be sorry to leave Stonyhurst; but go or stay, there is no likelihood of my ever doing anything to last. And I do not know how it is, I have no disease, but I am always tired, always jaded, though work is not heavy, and the impulse to do anything fails me or has

---

[26] *Letters*, II, p. 104.   [27] ibid., p. 105.

in it no continuance.'[28] Was already a nebulous feeling that he was, or would ultimately prove to be, 'Time's eunuch' gnawing him in the regions of the subconscious, producing in him this feeling of failure in the world? But, contrary to his expectations, Hopkins's appointment was renewed at the Stonyhurst College. He took a short holiday in August 1883 and spent some time at his father's and some more in Holland. He returned to Stonyhurst next month, and notwithstanding his almost 'spent powers', continued to discharge his duties to everybody's satisfaction except his own.

[28] *Letters*, I, p. 183.

X. HOPKINS AND DUNS SCOTUS

A LITTLE incident that took place earlier in Hopkins's life and which profoundly influenced his attitude to Nature, or rather agreeably confirmed his attitude, might be separately dealt with here. There is this significant entry in the Journal under date August 1872: 'After the examinations we went for our holiday out to Douglas in the Isle of Man August 3. At this time I had first begun to get hold of the copy of Scotus on the *Sentences* in the Baddely library and was flushed with a new stroke of enthusiasm. It may come to nothing or it may be a mercy from God. But just then when I took in any inscape of the sky or sea I thought of Scotus.'[1] The Scotus here referred to is, of course, the famous Duns Scotus, and 'on the *Sentences*' is his celebrated commentary on the *Sentences* of Peter Lombard, a noted theological work. Scotus, the thirteenth-century scholastic and Franciscan, was henceforth to shape Hopkins's philosophical views and encourage him to go his own way in his apprehension of Nature's beauties and their realization in poetry. In due course Hopkins met other enthusiasts of Scotus. On 27 August 1873, Hopkins wrote in his Journal: 'I walked with Herbert Lucas by the river and talked Scotism with him for the last time.'[2] Again, on 9 July 1874, he noted: 'I met Mr David Lewis, a great Scotist, and at the same time old Mr Brande Morris was making a retreat with us: I got to know him, so that oddly I made the acquaintance of two and I suppose the only two Scotists in England in one week.'[3] Months passed, but Hopkins's

---

[1] *Note-Books*, p. 161.   [2] ibid., p. 182.
[3] ibid., p. 198.

interest in Scotus only grew still more, and next year he actually wrote to Bridges: 'It was with sorrow I put back Aristotle's Metaphysics in the library some time ago feeling that I could not read them now and so probably should never. After all I can, at all events a little, read Duns Scotus and I care for him more even than Aristotle and more *pace tua* than a dozen Hegels.'[4]

Why, then, was Hopkins thus irresistibly attracted towards Scotus? Jesuits are followers of St Thomas Aquinas, though not such literal followers as most of the Dominicans. But, though separated by several centuries, Hopkins discovered in Scotus, rather than in St Thomas, a surprisingly kindred soul.[5] He had been feeling now and then, rather guiltily perhaps, that his sensuous awareness of Nature's hues and tonal connotations was a piece of foreign matter in his Jesuitical composition: but Scotus reassured him, and convinced him that he could revel in Nature and yet be strictly and wholly a Christian. The inelegant, unpoetical reflections of Scotus nevertheless acquired in Hopkins's eyes unique fascination and authority. 'Scotus was not a poet, and Hopkins was not therefore as a poet his disciple, but Scotus was a philosopher, and in so far as Hopkins became a philosopher, he became a Scotist': thus Mr Daniel Sargent.[6] It is perhaps better to put it this way: Hopkins became, unconsciously it may be, a Scotist philosopher finding in Scotism a justification for his own poetical sensuousness and inescapable awareness of the objective world.

---

[4] *Letters*, I, p. 31.
[5] One can, of course, be a follower of Aquinas without being a 'Thomist' in the strict sense. Suarez, the chief Jesuit interpreter of St Thomas, disagrees with him in many points. Hence there was nothing very extraordinary in Hopkins feeling the attraction of Scotus. (*vide* Pick's *Gerard Manley Hopkins*, pp. 156-9.)
[6] *Four Independents*, p. 157.

Scotism gives as high a place to abstract knowledge as does Thomism, but, unlike Thomism, it leaves the door open—and invitingly open—for a direct knowledge of objective reality: and this had been the very aim and front of Hopkins's poetical experiments during this period of his life. St Bonaventure had spoken of certain vestiges or traces of God that are clearly enough visible in Nature to those who would see. The vestiges are witnesses to God's undying glory and illimitable grace; they are spiritual telescopes bringing to our ken what otherwise our naked eyes would have missed. Already, with his complicated terminology of 'instresses' and 'inscapes', Hopkins was inventing his own soul's telescopes to discover to himself and to exhibit to others His eternal Glory: but when he found that Duns Scotus had spoken, several centuries earlier, of certain *formalitates* that possess the efficacy of revealing to the mind the particular, individual thing in relation to the whole and also the purpose behind the whole, Hopkins wondered if he had not received most unexpected corroboration from an unimpeachable authority for his own half-formed intuitions and beliefs. Scotus had found himself 'set down in a world of created substances; and he must first acquire a knowledge of these if he is to rise to that of the Ideas; he cannot possibly install himself in the world of Ideas and look down complacently from that height on the world of bodies.'[7] No; Hopkins would not shut his eyes to the teeming abundance of Nature around him: as he wrote in 'Inversnaid'—

> Degged with dew, dappled with dew
> Are the groins of the braes that the brook treads through,
> Wiry heathpacks, flitches of fern,
> And the beadbonny ash that sits over the burn.

[7] Etienne Gilson, *The Spirit of Medieval Philosophy* (English Trans. by A. H. C. Downes, Sheed & Ward, 1936), p. 241.

What would the world be, once bereft
Of wet and wildness? Let them be left,
O let them be left, wildness and wet;
Long live the weeds and the wilderness yet.[8]

Not of inanimate Nature only, of beasts and flowers and rocks and plains; men and women, too, the young not least, interested Hopkins. Thus of a brother and a sister—

She leans on him with such contentment fond
As well the sister sits, would well the wife;
His looks, the soul's own letters, see beyond,
Gaze on, and fall directly forth on life.

But ah, bright forelock, cluster that you are
Of favoured make and mind and health and youth,
Where lies your landmark, seamark, or soul's star?
There's none but truth can stead you. Christ is truth.[9]

And thus of the bugler boy who received his first communion—

Here he knelt then in regimental red.
Forth Christ from cupboard fetched, how fain I of feet
    To his youngster take his treat!
Low-latched in leaf-light housel his too huge godhead . . .

How it does my heart good, visiting at that bleak hill,
When limber liquid youth, that to all I teach
    Yields tender as a pushed peach,
Hies headstrong to its wellbeing of a self-wise self-will![10]

Again, in 'Brothers' we have the same humanity, the same deep urge to harmonize the objective and subjective levels of one's being into a total unity of God-realization. It is in this manner that Scotism is able 'to carry the human

---

[8] *Poems*, No. 33.   [9] ibid., No. 54.   [10] ibid., No. 23.

intellect much nearer to God than Thomism'.[11] 'Brothers' concludes with this robust affirmation—

> Ah Nature, framed in fault,
> There's comfort then, there's salt;
> Nature, bad, base, and blind,
> Dearly thou canst be kind;
> There dearly thén, deárly,
> I'll cry thou canst be kind.[12]

Elsewhere Hopkins's welling faith in the instrinsic goodness of things and in the beauty of human faces is expressed in terms of universality—

> As kingfishers catch fire, dragonflies dráw fláme;
> As tumbled over rim in roundy wells
> Stones ring; like each tucked string tells, each hung bell's
> Bow swung finds tongue to fling out broad its name;
> Each mortal thing does one thing and the same . . . .
> . . . . Christ plays in ten thousand places,
> Lovely in limbs, and lovely in eyes not his
> To the Father through the features of men's faces.[13]

And the earth itself, 'sweet Earth, sweet landscape, with leaves throng and louched low grass', all this mighty world of eye and ear, 'canst but only be': but—

> . . . . what is Earth's eye, tongue, or heart else, where
> Else, but in dear and dogged man?[14]

This willingness to set his feet firmly on the solid earth, this eagerness to reconcile a profound and intangible other-worldliness with an unerring and pertinacious this-worldliness, was the direct outcome of a poet turned Jesuit, of a man of vision and a man of action being merged together.

---

[11] Gilson, *The Spirit of Medieval Philosophy*, pp. 264-5.
[12] *Poems*, No. 30.   [13] ibid., No. 34.
[14] ibid., No. 35.

The idea of God that might be distilled from Hopkins's poetry is, more or less, the Christian idea *vis-à-vis* the Greek idea, so appositely defined and contrasted in M. Etienne Gilson's Gifford Lectures:

'The Christian mental universe is distinguished from the Greek mental universe, by ever more and more profound structural differences. On the one side we have a god defined by a perfection in the order of quality: Plato's Good; or by a perfection in one of the orders of being: Aristotle's Thought; on the other side stands the Christian God Who is first in the order of being, and Whose transcendence is such that, in the vigorous phrase of Duns Scotus, when we have a first mover of this kind it needs more of a metaphysician to prove that He is first than it does of a physicist to prove that He is a mover.... On the Greek side, stands a universe contingent in the order of intelligibility or in the order of becoming; on the Christian side a universe contingent in the order of existence. On the Greek side, there is the immanent finality of an order interior to beings; on the Christian side the transcendent finality of a Providence who creates the very being of order along with that of the things ordered.'[15]

It is not enough, in exploring the problem of being, to intellectualize it and reach intelligibility; one must touch existence itself, even the brute article, brute-seeming dappled things and dear and dogged man. Hopkins saw Nature steadily, ecstatically, adoringly, even as Keats did; but Hopkins went further, and 'inscaped' Nature and saw it as a glorious vestige of the in-dwelling God.[16] And for achieving this the stimulus he received from Duns Scotus is as incalculable as it has been of great consequence to English poetry.

[15] *The Spirit of Medieval Philosophy*, p. 81.
[16] cf. Pick, p. 56: 'Thus it is that a Jesuit like Hopkins can be at the same time a priest true to heaven and a poet true to earth.'

Hopkins's interest in, and spiritual allegiance to Duns Scotus never wavered and never waned. In 1884 he wrote to Coventry Patmore that Scotus 'saw too far, he knew too much; his subtlety overshot his interests; a kind of feud arose between genius and talent, and the ruck of talent in the Schools finding itself, as his age passed by, less and less able to understand him, voted that there was nothing important to understand and so first misquoted and then refuted him.'[17] Hopkins also carried on a long and interesting correspondence with Dr Mandell Creighton (of which the latter's part is now available[18]) regarding the name and birthplace of Duns Scotus. It is unnecessary to enumerate all the passages in Hopkins's poetry that show the influence of Duns Scotus and his philosophy. Hopkins's most important poems, including 'The Wreck of the *Deutschland*', owe much of their fluidity and humanity to Duns Scotus. Twice Hopkins introduced Scotus directly into his poetry. The first instance occurs in 'The Loss of the *Eurydice*'—

>   Deeply surely I need to deplore it,
>   Wondering why my master bore it,
>   The riving off that race
>   So at home, time was, to his truth and grace
>
>   That a starlight-wender of ours would say
>   The marvellous Milk was Walsingham Way
>   And one—but let be, let be:
>   More, more than was will yet be.[19]

'*And one*' refers to Scotus; and the meaning of this rather obscure passage has been explained in a letter to Bridges: 'The island was so Marian that the very Milky Way we made

---

[17] *Letters*, III, pp. 201-2.   [18] ibid., pp. 271-7.
[19] *Poems*, No. 17, ll. 97-104.

a roadmark to that person's shrine and from one of our seats of learning[20].... went forth the first great champion of her Immaculate Conception, now in our days made an article of faith.'[21] Secondly, Hopkins embalmed his reverent gratitude to the memory of Scotus in a sonnet written on the occasion of a visit to Oxford University in 1879—

> .... this air I gather and I release
> He lived on; these weeds and waters, these walls are what
> He haunted who of all men most sways my spirits to peace;
>
> Of realty the rarest-veined unraveller; a not
> Rivalled insight, be rival Italy or Greece;
> Who fired France for Mary without spot.[22]

[20] i.e., Oxford. [21] *Letters*, I, p. 77.
[22] *Poems*, No. 20.

XI. POEMS ON MAN AND NATURE

In his Nature poetry, Hopkins betrayed as complete and unashamed a sensuousness as Keats himself; but the same Hopkins revealed also a Wordsworthian capacity to probe into Nature's deeper purposes and to bring out, though with a vital difference, her immense healing power. In some of his most characteristic and successful poems, like 'God's Grandeur' or 'Hurrahing in Harvest' or 'The Windhover' or the fragment 'On the Portrait of Two Beautiful Young People', Hopkins seems to be able to fuse a Keatsian immediacy of sense perception with the spiritual tranquillity of Wordsworth and his sublime healing power. Hopkins had read both Keats and Wordsworth, and was very well aware of their merits. Though he wrote of Keats to Patmore in seemingly disparaging terms, he was also alive to the promise of a different kind of poetry in Keats's later work: 'It is impossible not to feel with weariness how his verse is at every turn abandoning itself to an unmanly and enervating luxury.... His contemporaries, as Wordsworth, Byron, Shelley, and even Leigh Hunt, right or wrong, still concerned themselves with great causes, as liberty and religion; but he lived in mythology and fairyland the life of a dreamer. Nevertheless I feel and see in him the beginnings of something opposite to this, of an interest in higher things and of powerful and active thought.... His defects were due to youth....'[1] On the other hand, the 'wise passiveness' of Wordsworth was not Hopkins's way of communion with Nature. The perception in Nature of something unusual, or of something specially

[1] *Letters*, III, pp. 237-8.

striking in the usual, thrilled Hopkins; his sensuous faculties were alert and alive; he abandoned himself, for a time, to the sheer loveliness, the glory of the thing. Mark the agitated exclamations in 'The Starlight Night'—

> Look at the stars! look, look up at the skies!
> O look at all the fire-folk sitting in the air!
> The bright boroughs, the circle-citadels there!
> Down in dim woods the diamond delves! the elves'-eyes!
> The grey lawns cold where gold, where quickgold lies!
> Wind-beat whitebeam! airy abeles set on a flare!
> Flake-doves sent floating forth at a farmyard scare![2]

The intellectual conclusion, reinforcing Hopkins's religious faith, is poetically realized in the last three lines of the sonnet[3]—

> These are indeed the barn; withindoors house
> The shocks. This piece-bright paling shuts the spouse
> Christ home, Christ and his mother and all his hallows.

Again, though more subdued in tone, the sonnet 'Hurrahing in Harvest' was really 'the outcome of half an hour of extreme enthusiasm as I walked home alone one day from fishing in the Elwy';[4] the poem is an unforgettable and exhilarating galvanization of Autumn—

> Summer ends now; now, barbarous in beauty, the
>   stooks arise
> Around; up above, what wind-walks! what lovely
>   behaviour
> Of silk-sack clouds! has wilder, wilful-wavier
> Meal-drift moulded ever and melted across skies?

[2] *Poems*, No. 8.
[3] cf. Fr M. C. D'Arcy, S. J.: 'We see the change-over in maturity: the pre-occupation with the true "scape" of things designed by God, the sense of the passing loveliness of earthly things and the need of dedicating them through the Cross to Christ.' (Foreword to Pick, *Gerard Manley Hopkins*.)
[4] *Letters*, I, p. 56.

> I walk, I lift up, I lift up heart, eyes,
>   Down all that glory in the heavens to glean our
>   Saviour....⁵

Though the immediate necessity is to gain emotional relief by giving expression to his tingling exhilarations, the central aim of his dedicated life is not, and cannot be, forgotten. To 'glean our Saviour! That is ever the purpose, the mainspring, the trembling essence of his poetry. It is so in 'Spring'; the sensibility of the poet is laced by Christian thought, but ever so unobtrusively—

> Nothing is so beautiful as spring—
>   When weeds, in wheels, shoot long and lovely and lush;
>   Thrush's eggs look little low heavens, and thrush
> Through the echoing timber does so rinse and wring
> The ear, it strikes like lightnings to hear him sing;
>   The glassy peartree leaves and blooms, they brush
>   The descending blue; that blue is all in a rush
> With richness; the racing lambs too have fair their fling.

This vivid piece of description is followed by the sestet that clearly betrays 'the confessor's care of souls'—

> What is all this juice and all this joy?
>   A strain of the earth's sweet being in the beginning
> In Eden garden....⁶

Robert Bridges, talking of 'The Leaden Echo and the Golden Echo', expressed his disapproval of the 'naked encounter of sensualism and asceticism' which 'hurts' the poem.⁷ In Hopkins's mature poems of Nature there is indeed an encounter, not of sensualism and asceticism, but of sensuous awareness and intuitional faith. 'God's Grandeur'

---

⁵ *Poems*, No. 14.   ⁶ ibid., No. 9.   ⁷ ibid., p. 96.

is an affirmation of objective beauty—a beauty that by its very presence reveals an even finer spiritual reality—

> The world is charged with the grandeur of God.
> It will flame out, like shining from shook foil;
> It gathers to a greatness, like the ooze of oil
> Crushed . . . .
>
> And for all this, nature is never spent;
> There lives the dearest freshness deep down
> things . . .
> Because the Holy Ghost over the bent
> World broods with warm breast and with ah!
> bright wings.[8]

It is noteworthy that the sustaining idea of this sonnet occurs also in Hopkins's 'Comments on the Spiritual Exercises of St Ignatius Loyola': 'The last mystery meditated on in the Spiritual Exercises is our Lord's Ascension . . . it is the contemplation of the Holy Ghost sent to us through creatures. . . . All things therefore are charged with love, are charged with God and if we know how to touch them give off sparks and take fire, yield drops and flow, ring and tell of him.'

Even more characteristic is the exquisite anthology-piece, 'Pied Beauty', in which through a brilliant enumeration of a series of contrasts is forged the simple sublime of the conclusion; by cataloguing the seeming dichotomies Hopkins would hymn their final integration in God who eternally embodies the principle of identity in difference, of agreement in disagreement—

> Glory be to God for dappled things—
> For skies of couple-colour as a brinded cow;
> For rose-moles all in stipple upon trout that swim;

[8] *Poems*, No. 7.

> Fresh-firecoal chestnut-falls; finches' wings;
>   Landscape plotted and pieced—fold, fallow, and plough;
>   And áll trádes, their gear and tackle and trim.
> All things counter, original, spare, strange;
>   Whatever is fickle, freckled (who knows how?)
>   With swift, slow; sweet, sour; adazzle, dim;
> He fathers-forth whose beauty is past change:
>   Praise him.⁹

The music of this poem is irresistible when it is read with understanding, and yet Mr Greening Lamborn brands it 'of the primitive kind'. But even he, though he has several hard things to say of this poem, considers that 'the metaphor of the fresh firecoal is a flash of poetic genius by which we see the chestnut as something rich and strange, "burning bright", illustrating Shelley's saying that the function of poetry is to make familiar objects to be as if they were not familiar'.¹⁰ To Hopkins Nature is an enchanted integration of pied beauty. Things in Nature tantalize us, adazzle us by their variety and complexity. But varied, shifting, pied as things are, their 'Creator' Himself is One; He is changeless, eternal. It is poems like these that Mr Sargent has in mind when he says that Hopkins 'used Nature as the phraseology of his poetry, and he did not sacrifice God in doing it'.¹¹ And it is of such poems that Canon Dixon wrote: 'In the power of forcibly and delicately giving the essence of things in nature, and of carrying one out of one's self with healing, these poems are unmatched.'¹² Elsewhere, Dixon speaks of Wordsworth's healing power, and adds that

---

⁹ *Poems*, No. 13.
¹⁰ *Poetic Values* (Oxford University Press, 1928), p. 201.
¹¹ *Four Independents*, p. 145. cf. Pick, p. 55 : ' "Pied Beauty" and the other poems of this group—indeed all that Hopkins ever wrote—are the poet's *Laudate Dominum* in which he calls on all creation to praise their Creator.'
¹² *Letters*, II, p. 32.

this is 'perhaps the best quality of poetry'.¹³ Wordsworth's healing power is quietly aglow in both his Nature poems and in those poems in which he tried to vivify the primary human emotions as evidenced in the lives of the common folk. Hopkins had great admiration for Wordsworth, and, in his own unique way, he tried to follow in the footsteps of the older poet.

On 14 August 1879 we find Hopkins writing to Bridges: 'I find within my professional experience now a good deal of matter to write on. I hope to enclose a little scene that touched me at Mount St Mary's. It is something in Wordsworth's manner; which is, I know, inimitable and unapproachable, still I shall be glad to know if you think it a success, for pathos has a point as precise as jest has and its happiness "lies ever in the ear of him that hears, not in the mouth of him that makes".'¹⁴ The poem here alluded to is 'Brothers' to which reference has already been made in an earlier chapter. Later, Hopkins made further comments on the poem: 'It was first written in stanzas in Wordsworth's manner, but when I compared it with his inimitable simplicity and gravity I was disgusted and meant to destroy it, till the thought struck me of changing the metre, which made it do.'¹⁵ 'Brothers' is the successful rendering of the emotion that perennially bubbles forth unseen, unnoticed in the lives of two brothers; one of them registers a series of triumphs, the other shares the joy without fret or envy—

> For, wrung all on love's rack,
> My lad, and lost in Jack,
> Smiled, blushed, and bit his lip;
> Or drove, with a diver's dip,

---

[13] *Letters*, II, p. 144. [14] *Letters*, I, p. 86.
[15] ibid., p. 106.

POEMS ON MAN AND NATURE

> Clutched hands down through clasped knees—
> Truth's tokens tricks like these,
> Old telltales, with what stress
> He hung on the imp's success.[16]

Similarly, in 'Spring and Fall: to a Young Child' Hopkins delicately unfolds a child's growing sensibility. Young Margaret grieves because the trees in the grove are getting leafless and beauty is fading away. Sorrow is, after all, one of the badges of our limitation; even a simple child 'that lightly draws its breath' should know—she would know by and by—that 'sorrow's springs are the same':

> It is the blight man was born for,
> It is Margaret you mourn for.[17]

Hopkins could have merely sentimentalized over the child's grief—but he would not; not out of ignorance, but through knowledge illumined by grace, could real happiness evolve. This Wordsworthian sympathy towards Nature and all living creatures, old and young, proud and wretched alike, is further exemplified in poems like 'Felix Randal' and 'Harry Ploughman', and even in a fragment like 'Cheery Beggar'; these characters are kin to Wordsworth's leech gatherer, old Cumberland beggar, Michael, and the rest. Felix Randal was only a farrier, but his death is of momentous significance to Hopkins. This 'mould of man, big-boned and hardy-handsome' was broken by sickness, 'fatal four disorders'—and admiringly, sorrowingly, and consolingly Hopkins sings the dirge—

> This seeing the sick endears them to us, us too it endears.
> My tongue had taught thee comfort, touch had
>   quenched thy tears,
> Thy tears that touched my heart, child, Felix, poor
>   Felix Randal;

---

[16] *Poems*, No. 30.   [17] ibid., No. 31.

> How far from then forethought of, all thy more
> boisterous years,
> When thou at the random grim forge, powerful amidst
> peers,
> Didst fettle for the great drayhorse his bright and
> battering sandal! [18]

The 'Cheery Beggar' is also convincingly individualized in the eight lines of the fragment that has happily survived; beyond Magdalen and by the Bridge the Beggar used to be seen—

> The motion of that man's heart is fine
> Whom want could not make pine, pine
> That struggling should not sear him, a gift should cheer him
> Like that poor pocket of pence, poor pence of mine. [19]

And Harry the Ploughman, cast in humble slough, but every inch a man; he is humanity itself, brave, struggling, using all its might in the fulfilment of its elementary duties: Hopkins's picture of this tiller of the soil is forcibly vivid—

> Hard as hurdle arms, with a broth of goldish flue
> Breathed round; the rack of ribs; the scooped flank; lank
> Rope-over thigh; knee-nave; and barrelled shank—
> Head and foot, shoulder and shank—
> By a grey eye's heed steered well, one crew, fall to;
> Stand at stress. Each limb's barrowy brawn, his thew
> That onewhere curded, onewhere sucked or sank—
> Soared or sank . . . .
>
> He leans to it, Harry bends, look. Back, elbow, and
> liquid waist
> In him, all quail to the wallowing o' the plough. [20]

It is as though a Velazquez or an El Greco has taken to writing poetry instead of painting portraits—so inescapably

---

[18] *Poems*, No. 29.   [19] ibid., No. 61.
[20] ibid., No. 43.

are these characters implicated in our consciousness. There is little that one can do so long as all one's faculties—physical, intellectual, spiritual—are not harnessed to the task in one supreme organized endeavour, distilling pleasure from it whatever pain also there might be as well. Harry laboured hard, fearfully and fanatically hard, his mind and muscle and will fused into a huge engine of furious concentration; and yet it was this adventure of suffering that stormed the gates of felicity, and pain and delight were seen to be one and the same. Harry the Ploughman is the mute Karmayōgin whose work, being the body's offering to God, is akin to prayer: for, as Hopkins says elsewhere, 'it is not only prayer that gives God glory but work'.[21]

The dynamics of purposive action are even more thrillingly vivified in what is perhaps Hopkins's most perfect single poem, 'The Windhover'. This sonnet has been elaborately commented upon by various critics—Mrs Phare, Mr Empson, Dr Richards, Mr Herbert Read, Dr John Pick, to name no others. And yet it refuses to yield its secrets completely. Its magic, however, is a most potent thing, and one has merely to read it to come under its spell—

I caught this morning morning's minion, king-
  dom of daylight's dauphin, dapple-dawn-drawn Falcon,
                                          in his riding
Of the rolling level underneath him steady air, and
                                              striding
High there, how he rung upon the rein of a wimpling wing
In his ecstasy! then off, off forth on swing,
  As a skate's heel sweeps smooth on a bow-bend:
                              the hurl and gliding
  Rebuffed the big wind. My heart in hiding
Stirred for a bird,—the achieve of, the mastery of the thing![22]

---

[21] *Note-Books*, p. 304.   [22] *Poems*, No. 12.

The windhover, the falcon, rises at dawn and hovers in the air. The sight dazzles Hopkins and he snaps the bird as it battles against the wind and achieves a delicate balance in mid-air. Hopkins chooses incantatory words for the purpose and the octave is in consequence a piece of word-magic. 'My heart in hiding stirred for a bird'—this line has puzzled the critics and Freud has been commissioned to psycho-analyse the case of Father Hopkins. The line perhaps means no more than this: here is a bird, a mere diminutive falcon, and yet its mastery over the elements is so flawless and final; but Hopkins himself, though a man and as such the crown of creation, can do nothing with like completeness and finality—and must he not be in hiding for very shame? The sestet naturally falls into two halves—

Brute beauty and valour and act, oh, air, pride, plume, here
   Buckle! AND the fire that breaks from thee then, a billion
Times told lovelier, more dangerous, O my chevalier!

   No wonder of it: shéer plód makes plough down sillion
Shine, and blue-bleak embers, ah my dear,
   Fall, gall themselves, and gash gold-vermilion.

'Thee . . . O my chevalier!' Is it Hopkins addressing the bird or Christ addressing Hopkins? At the end of the octave, the poet's heart is 'in hiding stirred for a bird': it is therefore natural to suppose that Christ intervenes to console and exhort his 'chevalier', to place before him a nobler ideal than even 'success'. The crucial word is 'buckle'—which may mean 'get to work' or 'start vigorously'. Man should get to work mobilizing for the purpose all his faculties—physical, intellectual, spiritual—and the action that ensues is a sacrificial offering, 'a billion times told lovelier, more dangerous' than mere muscular display. And seeming defeat and destruction will resolve into a splendorous triumph, terrible and beautiful in its defiance of death. Nor is there anything surprising in this, for this is but one instance of the divine alchemy that transmutes tragedy into triumph and death into immortality.

Dr Pick, however, identifies 'chevalier' with the bird and construes 'buckle' as 'give way' or 'crumple up'. The windhover of a sudden is forced to dive down and break itself; and the fury of its self-destroying swoop is 'a billion times told lovelier, more dangerous' than its earlier ecstasy. When the plough breaks the earth, when sparks fly away from the hearth—always there is exceeding beauty in death, beauty that exceeds death itself and acquires immortality! Dr Pick draws the moral of the sonnet in terms of the Passion and the Resurrection: 'Here is Christ upon the Cross and Hopkins the *alter Christus*. Beautiful was Christ's public life, but "a billion times told lovelier" was His self-immolation on the Cross, His sacrifice transmuted by the Fire of Love into something far greater than any mere natural beauty. More beautiful than any natural achievement was Hopkins's own humble and plodding continuance of the ethic of redemption through his own mystical self-destruction. . . . And the beauty of Christ and the beauty of the Jesuit to eyes that see more than this world is the beauty of their dying to live.'[23]

Some critics complain that the last lines of 'The Windhover' are weak and signify the poet's exhaustion. After the feverish intensity of the experience that has gone into the first eleven lines, well may the poet's passion decline into a dying fall: and this too is integral to the scheme of the poem. In 'The Windhover' Hopkins did register at last 'the achieve of, the mastery of the thing'; and he humbly dedicated it to 'Christ our Lord'.

[23] Pick, p. 71.

XII. HOPKINS AND BRIDGES

THE late Arthur Clutton-Brock once differentiated between 'intimate' and 'long-distance' popularity. Of Hopkins it may be safely said that he did not, at any period of his life, enjoy 'long-distance' popularity. His name did not appear in the newspapers frequently; he made no triumphant tours, issuing statements, making pompous speeches on all subjects under the sun; and he published no books. First he was a student, and being no explosive revolutionary like Shelley, created no great sensation, acquired no notoriety. Since the twenty-fourth year of his life he led the necessarily simple life of a Jesuit priest, functioning as a mere link, now here now there, in the chain of the vast organization of the Society of Jesus. He just mixed teaching with his professional duties, and so passed his days in meditation and uncomplaining service, an obscure priest all told; but beneath the uniform of a Jesuit lay the smouldering fires of a singularly alive human being, eager to give light no less than delight to others. It was inevitable that this other Hopkins should have enjoyed 'intimate' popularity in its most unblemished kind. He had some ripe and rare friends, and these friends loved him, honoured and admired him. They corresponded when they could not meet; and, unfortunately for them all, they could not do much of either. But friendship like theirs, built on the granite of unselfish devotion, could bravely endure in spite of the absence of personal intercourse or even of regular correspondence. Hopkins had known some of these friends, like Robert Bridges and Baillie, from his Oxford days; others, like Canon Dixon and Coventry Patmore, he came to know much later, Patmore even later than

Dixon. Bridges was a practitioner, like Balfour, of philosophic doubt; Dixon was a Protestant priest; Baillie was a Scot of Presbyterian upbringing, a rationalist and a lawyer; and Patmore was a Catholic, but not a priest. Again, Patmore and Dixon were considerably older than Hopkins, and hence of Bridges as well. And yet, in spite of these vital differences in social position, religious faith and even in age, Hopkins exerted on all his friends an influence that was truly remarkable. The bonds that knit him to every one of his friends were tender, sincere without qualification, and enduring. They never talked about tolerance, but lived it; and in this little universe of friendship and stern intellectual comradeship, Hopkins functioned as the focal point, the source of order and of light in this incredible world, the moral and intellectual king whose words commanded respect and whose criticisms acquired the weight of a judgement or the colour of a prophecy that must surely be fulfilled. In the result, the exchange of pulses in the little world of 'Hopkins and his Circle' almost looks like the pointer readings in an exclusive late Victorian intellectual laboratory.

Since Hopkins became a Jesuit, his vocation made it almost impossible for him to meet his friends often; his heavy duties made even letter writing a difficult task. Dixon and Patmore met Hopkins but rarely. And yet this wonderful friendship grew from strength to strength. How, then, did this miracle happen, and, happening, persist to the discomfiture of the worldly-wise of all times? Hopkins's letters furnish the clue to this mystery. Hopkins was so rare a soul that to know him was to love him; he was so sensitive a man that if he wrote at all he could not help betraying himself in every word and all along. He wore his heart—and he was a Jesuit too!—on his sleeve; and hence to receive even a letter from him, like the first letter Dixon received, was to establish an immediate and permanent contact with that irresistible personality. Writing was in his blood; he poured into his writings the precious life-blood of his spirit. The author who writes for a colossal public dilutes his personality, thins it out, destroys its individuality; at length his pen moves on, and lip-love rattles much like a skeleton's bones. But Hopkins had no public in mind; he wrote for the few, and latterly he wrote to gain personal relief, and may be to prove yet once more to Bridges and Dixon and one or two others that the gifts they had inferred in him were perhaps really there; and of course, in true humility, he wrote also for Christ, the justest and best critic. Such a man could afford to be himself, courageously and wholly himself in every little scrap that he wrote: and that is why his letters, his note-books, not to mention his poems, tantalize us by their capacity to reveal every contour of their author's personality. Naturally, since Hopkins knew Bridges from his university days, the letters that passed between the two should prove the most illuminating. Unfortunately, though Hopkins's letters have come down to us, Bridges's are lost; it seems likely that the latter purposely destroyed them when they were returned to him after his friend's death. 'One side of this fruitful friendship, therefore,' writes Professor Claude Colleer Abbott, 'has to be deduced from what remains. That is a grave misfortune.'[1] On the other hand, it is reasonable to suppose that practically all the letters that passed between Hopkins and Dixon, and again between Hopkins and Patmore, have been rescued from oblivion. Hopkins's letters to Baillie, too, have survived. Our thanks are due to the monumental labours of Professor Abbott and the enterprise of the Oxford University Press for having made all these letters accessible to the

---

[1] *Letters*, I, Preface, p. vi.

students of English literature generally, and to the admirers of Gerard Manley Hopkins in particular. These letters portray Hopkins, the man and the poet, as no biographer or critic can ever hope to do. In these we are permitted to see him as he saw himself, and as his intimate friends, some of them brother poets, saw him, and so seeing him admired and loved him.

When Hopkins's correspondence was published, an American reviewer remarked, in a moment of supreme critical divination, that they are the letters that a man could have written if he had combined the intoxicating sensuousness of Keats and the intellectual brilliance of Samuel Butler, the author of *Erewhon*. The reviewer might have added—'and the moral earnestness of Cardinal Newman'. Hopkins himself, in a letter to Baillie, placed his finger on the precise merit of his own letters, if only by implication. 'The letter-writer,' he remarked, 'on principle does not make his letter only an *answer*; it is a work embodying perhaps answers to questions put by his correspondents but that is not its main motive. Therefore it is as a rule not well to write with a received letter fresh on you. I suppose the right way is to let it sink into you, and reply after a day or two.'[2] This was exactly Hopkins's practice. It took him some days to compose a letter; and some of these letters are serious compositions, full of discussions on literary, linguistical or other matters. The letters are Hopkins's unmistakably, no other person could have written them; at the same time, they are Victorian letters, letters written at a time when everybody believed in the importance of being earnest. There is no frivolity, no triviality, no commonplaceness in these letters; and yet again neither is there any avoidable pomposity, abstruseness, sleep-inducing

[2] *Letters*, III, p. 68.

moralizing; Hopkins's intellectual honesty and his soul's earnestness saved even the longest letters from the somnolence of tedium; the letters may be difficult, but they are not dull; Hopkins's sense of humour, albeit not of the explosive variety popularized in our times, not merely saved his letters from dryness, but raised them to the level of creative literature and criticism.

Some readers might think that as letters Hopkins's are failures, because they tell us so little about himself; they discuss other people's poetry line by line, minutely and fearlessly, but of himself they say scarcely anything at all! It is true Hopkins says little *about* himself—and why should he when the letters, whatever their subject matter, *are* himself? The modern writer, when he talks about himself or appears to talk about himself, usually exploits a mere fake personality, not the genuine, unique thing; for, which personality, however fine and however complex, can stand the process of self-revelation for hundreds of weeks of popular journalism? The pages are covered with trivialities and trifles, soap bubbles and chaff and grain—and do they help us at all to touch the real man? There is more to be learnt from disciplined, self-controlled but courageously honest work like Hopkins's than from all the 'personal' essays and letters that now flood the Press and the bookstalls.

Early in the course of their friendship, Bridges had to bear the shock of Hopkins's conversion to Catholicism. At the very time when the spiritual crisis in him was most acute, Hopkins paid a visit to Bridges; the latter observed that something was wrong with his friend, but desisted from making any inquiries which might further accentuate the pain. Hopkins alludes to this in a letter to the Rev. Urquhart: 'Fr. Bridges I hid it with difficulty while I stayed at Rochdale, till my going to Birmingham made con-

cealment useless. His kindness at that time when he did
not know what was the matter with me I perpetually thank
God for.'³ To Bridges himself he wrote: 'I can never thank
you enough for yr. kindness at that time. Notwithstanding
my anxiety, which on the day we filled the aquarium was
very great indeed, it gives me more delight to think of the
time at Rochdale than any other time whatever than I can
remember.'⁴ With scarce a changed note the letters continue even after Hopkins's conversion. The death of their
common friend, Dolben, leads to a characteristic exchange
of sentiments. There is a human, homely touch presently:
'You sometimes now address me by my Christian name and
I like it but I do not you by yours, for first it wd. not feel
natural to me and secondly it wd. be unnecessary, for your
surname is the prettier.'⁵ Later Hopkins writes, gently in a
complaining tone: 'Usen't you to call me by my Christian
name? I believe you did. Well if you did I like it better.'⁶

In 1871 Hopkins wrote a letter to Bridges giving out-
spoken expression to what looked like 'red' opinions; this
scandalized Bridges much more than Hopkins's conversion
or noviciate at Roehampton had done, and for the next two
years and more no letters passed between the two. Hopkins
must have felt it a blow, and sorrowed in silence. When
early in 1874 a review in a Journal showed that Bridges
had published a book of poems, Hopkins made this an
opportunity for writing to his friend again. 'I think, my
dear Bridges, to be so much offended about that red letter
was excessive.'⁷ This immediately overwhelmed Bridges,
and the correspondence continued thereafter, without any
break, till Hopkins's death. Bridges, however, was still
nervous lest his letters should be perused by the Jesuit

³ *Letters*, III, p. 16.   ⁴ *Letters*, I, p. 6.
⁵ ibid., pp. 21-2.   ⁶ ibid., p. 32.   ⁷ ibid., p. 29.

authorites in transit; but Hopkins quickly reassured him:
'As for your letters being opened—you made that an objection before, I remember—it is quite unreasonable and superstitious to let it make any difference. To be sure they are torn half open—and so for the most part as that one can see the letter has never been out of the envelope—but can a Superior have the time or the wish to read the flood of correspondence from people he knows nothing of which is brought in by the post? No doubt if you were offering me a wife, a legacy, or a bishopric on condition of leaving my present life, and someone were to get wind of the purpose of the correspondence, *then* our letters would be well read or indeed intercepted. So think no more of that.'[8]

From now onwards a reversible series of letters dealing with the minutiæ of poetic creation passes between the two poets. Hopkins is a friendly, but nevertheless a fearless, critic of his friend's poetry; he is prepared always to call a spade a spade; and Bridges, who should have done the same in his letters, must clearly have benefited by such painstaking criticisms. Suddenly, Hopkins is on the defensive: 'You say you don't like Jesuits. Did you ever see one?'[9] Meanwhile, Hopkins has cultivated Canon Dixon's friendship, and immediately contrives that his two friends shall read and appreciate each other's poetry. 'A poet is a public in himself',[10] Hopkins assures Bridges, and advises the latter to post a copy of his poems to Dixon.

Hopkins now decides to take a great risk: he gently treads on the dangerous ground of his friend's religious belief. 'You understand of course,' he wrote, 'that I desire to see you a Catholic or, if not that, a Christian or, if not that, at least a believer in the true God (for you told me something of your views about the Deity which were not as

[8] *Letters*, I, p. 32.   [9] ibid., p. 40.   [10] ibid., p. 59.

they should be.) . . . I feel it is very bold, as it is uncalled for, of me to have written the above. Still, if we care for fine verses how much more for a noble life!'¹¹ In this letter Hopkins specifically advised Bridges to cultivate the Christian habit of giving alms. Bridges presumably argued contra in his reply: and Hopkins's reply to the reply contains an apology followed by a further exhortation, which perhaps made no deeper impression on Bridges than the first. And then the correspondence pursues its accustomed course—with no more attempts at conversion on Hopkins's part.

The letters henceforth often take a triangular course. Bridges writes to Dixon a not over-enthusiastic letter about his poetry; Dixon writes to Hopkins in a tone of slight disappointment; and Hopkins writes to Bridges, thus completing the cycle: 'I wonder, by the by, what you can have said that fell short of expectation. Must be a covetous old canon; shd. think abt. his soul.'¹² And so the letters go to and fro, as full as ever of suggestions, counter-suggestions, defences, confessions, *ex cathedra* judgements on various men of letters dead and alive, and what not.

Perhaps in one of his letters Hopkins had criticized Bridges's poetry with more than his usual thoroughness— a thoroughness that threatened to destroy even Bridges's self-confidence. He asked Hopkins plainly if it was any use his going on writing poetry. Hopkins was alarmed, and wrote one of the most beautiful and moving letters in the entire series: 'I see your work to its very least advantage when it comes to me on purpose to be criticized. . . . It is just as if I had written it myself and were dissatisfied, as you know that in the process of composition one almost always is, before things reach their final form. . . . You seem

---

[11] *Letters*, I, pp. 60-61.   [12] ibid., p. 77.

to want to be told over again that you have genius and are a poet and your verses beautiful. . . . If I were not your friend I shd. wish to be the friend of the man that wrote your poems. They shew the eye for pure beauty and they shew, my dearest, besides, the character which is much more rare and precious. . . .'[13] In a later letter there is further praise: 'Style seems your great excellence, it is really classical. What fun if you were a classic! So few people have style, except individual style or manner—not Tennyson nor Swinburne nor Morris, not to name the scarecrow misbegotten Browning crew.'[14] The same Hopkins regrets elsewhere that Bridges should call Matthew Arnold Mr Kidglove Cocksure.[15] But he also confesses, with intent perhaps to cover similar lapses of his own: 'I have in me a great vein of blackguardry and have long known I am no gentleman; though I had rather say this than have it said.'[16]

The fascinating letters continue—but we are permitted to see only one half of this epistolary treat.[17] Once Hopkins takes his friend to task for a veneer of cynicism in his attitude towards certain serious matters: 'Without earnestness there is nothing sound or beautiful in character and that a cynical vein much indulged coarsens everything in us.'[18] In due course Bridges is engaged, and he informs Hopkins: the latter writes jubilantly: 'The secret is out: I too am engaged on examination papers. . . .'[19] Later: 'The reason of course why I like men to marry is that a single life is a difficult, not altogether a natural life; to make it easily

---

[13] *Letters*, I, pp. 94-6.   [14] ibid., p. 111.
[15] ibid., p. 172.   [16] ibid., p. 129.
[17] Mr Read's comment is as follows: 'Bridges has cautiously destroyed his side of the correspondence, but that very caution is significant. A man has not such a care for his reputation but from what we call a good conceit of himself . . . .' (*A Coat of Many Colours*, p. 163.)
[18] *Letters*, I, p. 148.   [19] ibid., p. 192.

manageable special provision, such as we have, is needed, and most people cannot have this.'[20] Hopkins recognizes 'the elegant and legible hand' on the addresses to be that of Bridges's fiancée;[21] and lastly there is the letter of congratulation and good wishes on the day of the marriage:

'MY DEAREST BRIDGES AND MY DEAR MRS BRIDGES,— This is to wish you the happiest of days tomorrow and all the blessings of heaven on that and all the days of your wedded life. I did not consider the mails; the consequence is that these wishes must, like the old shoe, be sent *after* you; but there is no harm in that if when they overtake you they ever after attend you. . . .'[22]

Two months later, Hopkins writes again: 'I was very glad you gave me some word of your married life; I wish it had been more. I have a kind of spooniness and delight over married people, especially if they say "my wife", "my husband", or shew the wedding ring.'[23] Several years afterwards, subsequent to a visit to Yattenden, Hopkins gave this superb compliment to Mrs Bridges: 'When I was last at Yattenden I had the impression I had never in my life met a sweeter lady than Mrs Bridges. You may wear a diamond on your finger and yet never have seen it in a side light, so I tell you.'[24]

In one of these letters Hopkins gives an interesting account of himself: 'The irises of the present writer's eyes are small and dull, of a greenish brown; hazel I suppose; slightly darker at the outer rims.

'His hair . . . is lightish brown, but not equable nor the same in all lights; being quite fair near the roots and upon the temples, elsewhere darker . . . and shewing quite fair in the sun and even a little tawny. It has a gloss. On the

[20] *Letters*, I, p. 194.
[22] ibid., p. 197.
[24] ibid., p. 264.
[21] ibid., p. 195.
[23] ibid., p. 198.

temples it sometimes appears to me white. I have a few white hairs, but not there.'²⁵ This vivid description of Hopkins's personal appearance must be as interesting and valuable to his admirers as it must have been to his correspondent.

Thus, truncated though their correspondence has become, enough remains of it to enable the reader to reconstruct fairly completely the splendid friendship that subsisted between Hopkins and Bridges, in which both gave and received freely in such a manner that the giving and the receiving blessed them both. Bridges gave up the practice of medicine to follow the profession of poetry; it was a happy choice, and time justified him, and he died full of honour and years. Hopkins's was a greater sacrifice; it meant almost the suppression, ruthless and remorseless, of the acutely sensitive poet that he knew he was. Almost, but not quite. He became a poet after all, and with Bridges's guarded appreciation he continued, though only fitfully, a poet. Hopkins was throughout perfectly conscious of his debt to Bridges; it had given him what no money can procure, love; and one of the very last things he wrote was a sonnet addressed to Bridges; and the latter, on his part, not less conscious of his own debt to his friend, prefixed to his edition of Hopkins's poems a tender sonnet to his memory, commending his 'plumage of far wonder and heavenward flight'.[26]

[25] *Letters*, I, p. 253.
[26] In the light of all this, the view held by Mr Herbert Read that Bridges was not worthy of Hopkins's friendship seems to be biased. Thus Mr Read: 'One wonders on what the friendship subsisted, so little were Hopkins's profoundest feelings appreciated by Bridges.... We can assume, therefore, that the attraction was instinctive, even physical.' (*A Coat of Many Colours*, p. 163.)

XIII. BAILLIE, DIXON AND PATMORE

LIKE Bridges, Alexander William Mowbray Baillie was also Hopkins's lifelong friend. A rationalist, a lawyer, a man with independent means, an Egyptologist and a linguist, Baillie had above all a genius for friendship, 'being able to sympathize with and comprehend almost anything, while never moving from his own most definite roots'.[1] Neither their religious nor political differences in any way affected the esteem and affection Hopkins and Baillie had for each other. Of this correspondence too only one side is now available, for Baillie's letters seem to have disappeared altogether.[2]

The first of the published letters from Hopkins to Baillie is dated 10 July 1863 and the last twenty-five years later; there is hardly any inexplicable break in the correspondence. One of the correspondents was a Jesuit and the other was a bachelor; both lived secluded lives, as far away as possible from the rattle and drive of modern civilized life. Baillie himself not being a poet, in his letters Hopkins could not at any great length discuss poetry. Hence this series of letters is less striking than the series of letters that Hopkins wrote to Bridges, or even to Dixon and Patmore; on the contrary, this series tells us more about Hopkins's political views and linguistic researches than do the other groups of letters.

The earlier letters, indeed, are full of gossip, confidences, and gay talk. Presently the tone changes to one of more self-controlled gravity, but a sense of humour is never

---

[1] Note by Miss Hannah in *Letters*, III, p. 288.
[2] *Letters*, III, Preface, p. v.

long absent, and this makes the letters interesting and hence very readable indeed. Once Hopkins gives a sly hint that may help us to infer at least the lower rim of Bridges's letters: 'I will end,' says Hopkins, 'as Bridges always does to me with saying I am well aware what a stupid letter this is.'[3] Another letter contains some remarks about Hopkins's sisters; Baillie had written saying that he had chanced to meet Hopkins's sister, and this is the reply: 'That sister of mine that you met, I do not know which of them it was. The eldest, Millicent, is given to Puseyism: she is what is called an out-sister of the Margaret Street Home. . . . Consequently she will be directed by some Ritualist, which are the worst hands she could fall into. . . . The second, Kate, is a sort of humourist. Grace, the youngest, is devoted to music, for which she has a great aptitude. You may perhaps see by this which it was you met.'[4]

Since Baillie spent practically all his time in London, there were comparatively more opportunities for him to meet Hopkins than for others. It is not unlikely that their hearts of controversy were unleashed whenever they met. After one such meeting Hopkins felt that he had used too strong language, and wrote unreservedly to withdraw the offending words: 'I believe I am writing chiefly to withdraw something I said at our last meeting, though if there had been nothing to withdraw still I ought to write; but blackguardry stamps my whole behaviour to you from first to last. Strong words are seldom much good and the more of heat the less of reason. The strong word I repent of using was that if ever there was a humbug it was Swedenborg. What I might reasonably have said (and what I really meant) was that Swedenborgianism (what a word!) is

---

[3] *Letters*, III, p. 83.   [4] ibid., p. 93.

humbug.'⁵ 'The amend is handsome', as Professor Abbott remarks, though in another connexion: 'more than one road leads to nobility.'⁶

As Hopkins grew older, as for long stretches of time he lived practically an exile in Ireland, letters from his friends became more and more a necessary tonic to stimulate him intellectually and refresh him on the emotional levels of his being. In a letter like the following the seeming raillery but hides a nameless suffering: 'I am afraid the effect of all this will be to make you say "A firm foot must be put down on this sort of thing AT ONCE", but if it makes you write so much the better. It is a great help to me to have someone interested in something (that will answer my letters), and it supplies some sort of intellectual stimulus. I sadly need that and a general stimulus to being, so dull and yet harassed is my life.'⁷

The remaining letters for the most part discuss either linguistics, especially Greek-Egyptian derivations, or Gladstone's Irish policy. But the mutual esteem and affection show no signs of diminution. In fact in the very year before his death, in what was perhaps the last letter he wrote, Hopkins reiterates his faith in the efficacy of affection: 'Now at your present age, much the same as mine, you are aware that affection, no matter from whom it comes, is a precious thing and not to be found at random.'⁸ Such an unflinching assertion of his faith in affection and friendship must have struck a responsive chord in Baillie, who too had loved his friend wisely and long. It is no wonder therefore that one of Baillie's 'greatest regrets in no longer believing

⁵ *Letters*, III, p. 104.
⁶ *Letters*, I, Introduction, p. xlvii.
⁷ *Letters*, III, pp. 116-17.
⁸ ibid., p. 143.

in a second life was that he wanted so badly "somewhere, somehow, to meet Gerard Hopkins again".[9]

Perhaps, though, the most lovable of Hopkins's friends was neither Bridges nor Baillie nor Patmore, but Richard Watson Dixon, a poet and a priest and a historian of the Church of England. It was this man who one day in June 1878 received an unusual letter from Fr Hopkins, a letter which deeply moved the older poet.[10] Dixon remembered the face of Hopkins, though he had only seen him as a boy at Highgate School nearly twenty years before. Dixon's gentleness and humility are revealed in his very first letter to Hopkins: 'I am ashamed of writing so much of myself: none is so conscious of my defects as I am. Let me rather regard with admiration the arduous and self-denying career which is modestly indicated in your letter and signature: and which places you so much higher in "Christ's Company" than I am.'[11] Thus began a remarkable correspondence, conducted on both sides with a uniform sympathy and understanding, which continued till the end of Hopkins's life.

It is impossible to decide whom to admire more—whether Hopkins for encouraging the older man, once almost his own teacher, to pursue the profession of poetry in spite of the neglect of the public, or Dixon for coaxing the Jesuit priest to publish his poetry in his own lifetime. The correspondence brings out the best in both of them; they are throughout themselves and yet are attracted to each other, and they derive no small solace from this extraordinary attachment. Hopkins is able to place his finger on the sensitive spot of Dixon's poetic life: 'Disappointment and humiliations embitter the heart and make an

---

[9] Note by Miss Hannah in *Letters*, III, p. 288.
[10] *Letters*, II, p. 4.   [11] ibid., p. 5.

aching in the very bones';[12] but he presently applies the efficacious balm of an appeal to the wisest of critics, Christ. Dixon is again moved to the depths, for Hopkins's way of looking at such things as literary fame comes 'with the force of a revelation'.[13]

The letters now pass to and fro at fairly regular intervals. Dixon has learnt that his friend too is a poet, has read the poems in manuscript, and has been very much moved by the Nature poems especially; this only makes his regret all the keener that Hopkins should not be *known* as a poet. He asks if he might give 'an abrupt footnote' about Hopkins in the next volume of his Church History; and he adds naively: 'You may think it odd for me to propose to introduce you into the year 1540, but I know how to do it. My object would be to awaken public interest and expectation in your as yet unpublished poems: or your recently published, if you think of publishing before that time.'[14] Of course, Hopkins would have none of it. Again, Dixon tried to get some of Hopkins's sonnets into Hall Caine's anthology of sonnets; this, too, thanks to Caine's inability to acclimatize himself to Hopkins's unconventionality, came to nothing. But Dixon did succeed in publishing one of his friend's poems in his *Bible Birthday Book*; and he also dedicated to 'the Reverend Gerard Hopkins' a 'small Daniel of lyrics'.[15] On the other hand, Hopkins contributed an illuminating critical note on Dixon to Thomas Arnold's *Manual of English Literature*.

The main topic perennially discussed in their correspondence is criticism of each other's poems, whether in print or in manuscript. Each accepted, whenever possible, the other's suggestions; and the appreciations were no less

[12] *Letters*, II, p. 9.
[13] ibid., p. 10.
[14] ibid., p. 27.
[15] ibid., p. 131.

valuable to them in encouraging them to go on writing poetry, regardless of applause from what Shelley called 'the polluting multitude'. To Dixon such appreciation as came from a profound and critically acute mind as Hopkins's was no luxury, but a positive necessity; under date 24 January 1881, he wrote to Hopkins: 'Thank you for your kind words of my own writings. They gave me comfort when I needed it much. I need it still, and they still give it.'[16] Hopkins, on his part, should have felt no small measure of gratitude to his friend for showing such generosity of understanding as in—'I can understand that your present position, seclusion, and exercises would give to your writings a rare charm—they have done so in those that I have seen: something that I cannot describe, but know to myself by the inadequate word *terrible pathos*— something of what you call temper in poetry: a right temper which goes to the point of the terrible; the terrible crystal.'[17] Nowhere else, and by nobody else, has the uniqueness of Hopkins's characteristic poetry been so illuminatingly suggested.

After many fruitless attempts and vain longings to meet each other, Hopkins and Dixon met at last in March 1882. On this occasion it was the older man who felt shy; the very extremity of his happiness made him feel uncomfortable, and he later wrote to Hopkins apologetically: 'I daresay I seemed "shy": I have an unfortunate manner: and am constantly told that I am too quiet: I have often tried to overcome it: but the effort is always apparent to those with whom I am, and never succeeds. You must therefore forgive it: it is not from want of feeling or affection.'[18] Hopkins knew it all right; and he wrote

[16] *Letters*, II, p. 45.   [17] ibid., p. 80.
[18] ibid., p. 104.

about the visit to both Dixon and Bridges in grateful terms.

And so the two priests felt drawn towards each other, understood and appreciated each other; they discussed the implications of Sprung Rhythm and the possibilities of the Sonnet as a literary form; they discussed the classics, they weighed in the delectable balance of criticism the merits and defects of a Carlyle, a Browning, a Tennyson; they urged each other to write, felt a pride in each other's poetical achievements, and they experienced a pang if either suffered a disappointment or a slight. When Dixon lost the election to the Chair of Poetry at Oxford, Hopkins wrote:

'But "life is a short blanket"—profoundest of homely sayings: great gifts and great opportunities are more than life spares to one man. It is much if we get something, a spell, an innings, at all. See how the great conquerors were cut short, Alexander, Caesar just seen. Above all Christ our Lord: his career was cut short and, whereas he would have wished to succeed by success—for it is insane to lay yourself out for failure, prudence is the first of the cardinal virtues, and he was the most prudent of men—nevertheless he was doomed to succeed by failure; his plans were baffled, his hopes dashed, and his work was done by being broken off undone. However much he understood all this he found it an intolerable grief to submit to it. He left the example: it is very strengthening, but except in that sense it is not consoling.'[19]

Here the man, and not alone the Jesuit priest, is speaking; and he is speaking from the heart as well as from the head; he offers no empty palliatives for the chronic disease of human disappointment—one symptom of which makes the whole world kin—but rather recognizes its

---

[19] *Letters*, pp. 137-8.

ravaging nature while citing the examples of others who have suffered likewise.

Of Hopkins's major friends only Coventry Patmore was a Catholic, and he too was a convert and had known the tribulations a convert must face during the religious crisis in his life and subsequent to the conversion. Hopkins had read Patmore's poetry and sincerely appreciated it long before he made the acquaintance of the poet himself. This was on the occasion of the speech day at Stonyhurst; Patmore was a distinguished visitor, and Hopkins was asked to look after the already venerable poet. They quickly became friends; Patmore saw at once that Hopkins was both a good critic of poetry and a good Jesuit priest. It was settled that Patmore should send Hopkins his earlier books of verse for detailed criticism against a new edition. Hopkins later regretted having so agreed to criticize so rare a master as Patmore: 'I feel,' wrote Hopkins, 'that the task I have undertaken is a dangerous and an over-honourable one and perhaps it was presumptuous to accept it: now however I must go through with it. . . As my business is now to find faults, not beauties, and as if I wanted to feature out my admiration I shd. have to adduce the volumes themselves, I want it to be taken as said.'[20] Much of the ensuing correspondence is swallowed up by Hopkins's criticisms of Patmore's poetry—and these criticisms range from the form and spirit of the poems to the intricate minutiæ of language. Hopkins criticizes fearlessly, and always with a minute particularity; but the older poet is not offended; he takes the criticisms to be, what indeed they are, 'the greatest praise my poetry has ever received'. Such honest and valid criticism makes Patmore feel almost inclined 'to begin to sing again, after I thought I had given over'.[21] His replies

[20] *Letters*, III, p. 151.   [21] ibid., p. 177.

breathe an extraordinary humility, almost out of character in a man like Patmore. He agrees with nearly all Hopkins's suggestions and will endeavour to adopt nearly all of them.[22] 'I agree with almost all your criticisms'; 'as usual I agree with most of your remarks, though I may not be able to act on all those'; such is the refrain. Even Mr D. S. MacColl, who years ago[23] attempted to prick 'the bubble so assiduously blown round Hopkins' mistaken views on Prosody', had to make the half-hearted admission: 'Hopkins had fine qualities, however, as a critic of other men's verse, both technically and on points of moral implication, and Patmore had the rare sense and magnanimity to listen to the younger man and profit by many of his suggestions.'[24]

Though in the main Hopkins's criticisms touch only Patmore's choice of words and occasionally his prosody, there is one notable instance where the priest's objections are based on purely moral grounds. Hopkins had understood one of Patmore's poems to be a defence of vanity in women. This stings Hopkins to the quick, and he writes zealously and feelingly: 'It seems to me we shd. in everything side with virtue, even if we do not feel its charm, because good is good. . . . If modesty in women mean two things at once, purity and humility, must not the pair of opposites be no great way apart, vanity from impurity?'[25] Patmore explains his own connotation of the word 'vanity', but admits: 'it is a serious fault if the passage in question leaves such an impression as it does on your mind.'[26] Hopkins too makes amends: 'I must have read your lines in too gross a mood.'[27]

[22] *Letters*, III, p. 177.
[23] *The London Mercury*, July 1938, p. 217.
[24] ibid., p. 221. [25] *Letters*, III, p. 160.
[26] ibid., p. 163. [27] ibid., p. 164.

That Hopkins admired Patmore's poetry, and admired it a great deal, cannot be in question at all. It pained Hopkins that Patmore should be so little known; alluding to some of Patmore's best poems, Hopkins wrote: 'I sigh to think that it is all one almost to be too full of meaning and to have none and to see very deep and not to see at all, for nothing so profound as these can be found in the poets of this age, scarcely of any; and yet they are but little known and when the papers give a list of the contemporary English poets your name does not appear.'[28] On the other hand, Patmore was almost wholly unable to appreciate the poetry of Hopkins. The older poet could and did plead extenuating circumstances: 'I am conscious of my extreme slowness in taking fully in what is new. I suppose it comes of my all along having followed a single line of my own.'[29] The judgement itself, when it was actually delivered, must have disappointed Hopkins, the more so because at one time it must have appeared only too just to most conventionally minded persons. 'System and learned theory are manifest in all these experiments; but they seem to me to be *too* manifest'[30]—this was the verdict. Hopkins knew that the game was up; he wrote to Bridges in a tone of resignation: 'Mr Patmore did not on the whole like my poems, was unconverted to them.'[31] It was a little consoling, however, to be told that Bridges at any rate had roused Patmore to an ecstasy of admiration by 'getting through thousands and thousands of highly finished verses.'[32] Patmore felt wretched that he had to confess his inability to appreciate Hopkins as a poet; but conscientiously he could have done nothing else.

[28] *Letters*, III, p. 201.
[29] ibid., p. 204.
[30] ibid. p. 205.
[31] *Letters*, I, pp. 191-2.
[32] *Letters*, III, pp. 208-9.

But Patmore loved, almost revered, the man, the critic and the Jesuit priest. 'I assure you that I shall always regard my having made your acquaintance as an important event of my life, and there are few things I desire more than a renewal of opportunity of personal intercourse with you.'[33] Again: 'Your letters are always very encouraging, and really I sometimes require a little encouragement, considering the way I get treated by the fashionable critics.'[34] And soon after: 'your letters are quite events in my life of a hermit.'[35] And so on; both before and after Hopkins's death, Patmore was unwearying in stressing the nobility and goodness of his friend's character. As Professor Abbott beautifully concludes his excellent introduction to the third volume of Hopkins's correspondence: 'Though Patmore failed to understand the worth of the poet, no one discerned more clearly or stated more emphatically what was, for Hopkins, his crown of endeavour, the prevailing goodness of the priest.'

And yet, in one respect, Hopkins has left a wounded name in regard to his relations with Patmore. The latter's admirers are severe with Hopkins for what is described as his interference with the older poet's work. Thus Mr Derek Patmore: 'On several occasions Patmore bowed quite unnecessarily to the dogmatic opinions of the Jesuit.'[36] The published correspondence, however, tells a different tale; Hopkins criticized because he was nearly forced to do so; it was a labour of love, no less. Patmore's own letters breathe nothing but gratitude and affection for the younger critic; and as for the Jesuit's dogmatisms one searches for them in vain in the published correspondence.

[33] *Letters*, III, p. 216.   [34] ibid., p. 220.
[35] ibid., p. 223.
[36] Introduction to *Selected Poems of Coventry Patmore* (Chatto and Windus, Phoenix Edition) p. xxx.

A more serious charge, first framed by Edmund Gosse and since then repeated among others by Mr Derek Patmore, is that Coventry Patmore destroyed his *magnum opus*, a work in prose entitled *Sponsa Dei*, after Hopkins had passed certain strictures on it. Mr Derek Patmore writes: 'Hopkins disapproved of the work and told Patmore that it ought to be burnt, saying: "That's telling secrets." He gave him the alternative of showing it to his religious director. Patmore's pride rebelled against this, and he burnt the manuscript.'[37] The published correspondence proves without a shadow of doubt that Hopkins did not certainly advise that the book should be burnt, that Patmore did consult his director, and that the book was burnt over two years after Hopkins had passed the alleged remark. Professor Abbott rightly comes to the conclusion that Patmore burnt the manuscript 'because he himself was convinced that he ought to burn it'.[38]

Unfortunately Patmore was largely responsible for causing much of this misunderstanding, though critics of the calibre of Gosse and Osbert Burdett ought not to have taken him at his word but weighed all the available evidence before fixing the guilt on the Jesuit priest. Wishing only to praise Hopkins, and especially Hopkins's supreme *goodness*, Patmore wrote: 'The *authority* of his goodness was so great with me that I threw the manuscript of a little work—a sort of "Religio Poetae"—into the fire, simply because, when he had read it, he said with a grave look, "that's telling secrets." This little book had been the work of ten years' continual meditations, and could not but have made a greater effect than all the rest I have written; but his

---

[37] Introduction to *Selected Poems of Coventry Patmore*, p. xxxii.
[38] *Letters*, III, Introduction, p. xxxv.

doubt was final with me.'³⁹ Besides, he wrote on 10 February 1888 to Hopkins, insinuating that the responsibility for the burning of the manuscript lay ultimately with him. Hopkins was shaken to the roots; he wrote a reply of some length, but cancelled it; wrote again on 6 May, politely but none the less firmly, repudiating the charge: 'Your news was that you had burnt the book called *Sponsa Dei,* and that on reflection upon remarks of mine. I wish I had been more guarded in making them. When we take a step like this we are forced to condemn ourselves: either our work shd. never have been done or never undone, and either way our time and toil are wasted—a sad thought; though the intention may at both times have been good. My objections were not final, they were but considerations . . . even if they were valid, still if you had kept to yr. custom of consulting your director, *as you said you should,* the book might have appeared with no change or with slight ones. But now regret is useless.'⁴⁰ Nothing could be more to the point. There is no hint that the burnt manuscript was really Patmore's *magnum opus*; in writing it or in destroying it Patmore had done a regrettable thing, but anyhow the responsibility was wholly his. In his reply Patmore wrote that he did consult Dr Rouse, his director, but 'he seemed to have no strong opinion one way or another, but said that he thought that all the substance of the work was already published in my poems and in one or two of my papers. . . . So I felt free to do what your condemnation of the little book inclined me to do.'⁴¹ It is clear from all this that the charge against Hopkins cannot be sustained and that strictly the world has not lost much by the destruction

---

[39] Chapneys, *Memoirs and Correspondence of Coventry Patmore* (1890), Vol. II, p. 249.
[40] *Letters*, III, p. 237.   [41] ibid., p. 242.

of *Sponsa Dei*. But, then, prejudices die hard—and Hopkins's name has been too long under a cloud in this connexion. The publication of the correspondence of the two poets should finally help to clear the sky.

XIV. HOPKINS'S POLITICAL VIEWS

THE question might be asked: What were Hopkins's political views—or had he any? Hopkins was a Jesuit, not a politician; a poet, not a political theorist. And yet politics implicate every citizen, and no one can help thinking occasionally about the politics of one's country. Hopkins came of a family of respectable true-British Tories, but he was also a man of super-sensitiveness and sensibility. The term 'Tory' could not circumscribe him, nor any other single label; for, like all poets, he was large, he contained many things, and was ultimately and challengingly himself. But in some of his letters to his correspondents he has given his estimates of various statesmen and his opinions on current political problems; and even some of his poems seem to be written under the stress of what may not inaccurately be called his political convictions.[1] In a letter written to Bridges in 1871, Hopkins calls himself 'in a manner' a Communist, and continues: 'Their ideal bating some things is nobler than that professed by any secular statesman I know of. . . . Besides it is just.—I do not mean the means of getting to it are. But it is a dreadful thing for the greatest and most necessary part of a very rich nation to live a hard life without dignity, knowledge, comforts, delight, or hopes in the midst of plenty —which plenty they make. . . . England has grown hugely wealthy but this wealth has not reached the working classes; I expect it has made their condition worse.'[2] Hopkins fears that the working classes, in their just fury, may destroy not

---

[1] cf. Pick, p. 113: 'While we must not think of his political interests as being one of his heaviest crosses, yet they did form a very real part of his outlook.'
[2] *Letters*, I, pp. 27-8.

merely the material engine of Capitalism (he does not, of course, use the word) but also the old religion, the heritage of art and literature, and all 'the history that is preserved in standing monuments'. But, then, 'as the working classes have not been educated they know next to nothing of all this and cannot be expected to care if they destroy it'. The Hopkins of this letter is very like the Hopkins who once realized with a shudder that his mind was nearer to Walt Whitman's than to any other's[3]; and it is certainly the Hopkins who stuffed into the narrow mould of 'Tom's Garland' the incalculable implications of his views on the unemployed.

'Tom's Garland' is one of Hopkins's very obscure poems; Bridges found himself unable to get at its meaning, and hence Hopkins was compelled to supply an annotation. Though it is but a poem of twenty lines, with surprising compression and allusiveness it passes in review before our eyes the working man's daily double, double toil and trouble, his indispensable services to the Commonwealth, his return home and his relaxation, his pleasure and pride in his hard labour; but this is not all. In modern times, the working man is doubly lost—lost to himself and lost to the nation. Has not Professor Pigou said that the unemployed tends to become ultimately unemployable? Hopkins is convinced that the evils of the modern world are largely of our own creation. Hard labour, in itself, is not a thing to be disparaged; it is first without a second; but, adds Hopkins, 'presently I remember that this is all very well for those who are in, however low in, the Commonwealth and share in any way the Common weal; but that the curse of our times is that many do not share it, that they are outcasts from it and have neither security nor splendour; that they

---

[3] *Letters*, I, p. 155.

share care with the high and obscurity with the low, but wealth and comfort with neither. And this state of things, I say, is the origin of Loafers, Tramps, Cornerboys, Roughs, Socialists and other pests of society.'[4] The following is the picture of Tom, symbol of work and honest and low service—

> Tom—garlanded with squat and surly steel
> Tom; then Tom's fallowbootfellow piles pick
> By him and rips out rockfire homeforth—sturdy Dick;
> Tom Heart-at-ease, Tom Navvy; he is all for his meal
> Sure, 's bed now.

But in the modern world civilization has set up an inverted pyramid—and the many go without bread, without honour; they can work, but have no work; the dangers they share with the rich and the powerful, but share neither the glory nor the means of living—

> . . . Undenizened, beyond bound
> Of earth's glory, earth's ease, all; no one, nowhere,
> In wide the world's weal; rare gold, bold steel, bare
>   In both; care, but share care—
> This, by Despair, bred Hangdog dull; by Rage,
> Manwolf, worse; and their packs infest the age.[5]

Hopkins inevitably included the 'Socialists' among the 'pests of society', but his sympathy for the poor down-trodden is both manly and unmistakable, as for instance poems like 'Harry Ploughman' and 'Felix Randal' show. Such sympathetic portraits of working men and fearless manifestoes on their behalf like 'Tom's Garland' reveal a characteristically 'modern' or even a post-War consciousness lurking under-

---
[4] *Letters*, I, pp. 273-4.
[5] *Poems*, No. 42.

neath a mid-Victorian Jesuit uniform.⁶ The sufferings of
the poor—and Hopkins's priestly work brought him often
into intimate contact with them—pained him deeply and
left a deep scar; he disliked towns, and the misery of the
people in towns; 'the dirt, squalor, and the illshapen
degraded physical (putting aside moral) type of so many of
the people' injected him with 'the deeply dejecting, unbearable thought that by degrees almost all our population will
become a town population and a puny unhealthy and
cowardly one'.⁷ Again, 'my Liverpool and Glasgow experience laid upon my mind a conviction, a truly crushing conviction, of the misery of town life to the poor and more than
to the poor, of the misery of the poor in general, of the degradation even of our race, of the hollowness of this century's
civilization: it made even life a burden to me to have daily
thrust upon me the things I saw.'⁸ To have seen and felt
to the very marrow of his bones all that squalor and evil
heritage of wretchedness was to have suffered an almost
complete abridgement of his hopes; but though he staggered
Hopkins did not lose altogether his balance; faith saved him
from despair.

Though a Tory, then, Hopkins was a Tory like Disraeli, to whom three things were politically sacred: the
integrity of British Institutions, the safety of the Empire,
and the well-being of the people. Toryism was identifying
oneself with the nation, the people and the Empire as a
whole, and not merely with the middle classes—which,
according to Tory spokesmen like Disraeli, was Whiggism

---

⁶ It is, of course, inappropriate to use the word communism
in connexion with the social ideas of Hopkins. They are very
advanced, but by no means unorthodox. Most of them, in
fact, are in *Rerum Novarum,* encyclical of Leo XIII, published
in 1891.
⁷ *Letters*, III, p. 146. ⁸ *Letters*, II, p. 97.

or even Gladstonian Liberalism! Hopkins therefore loses few opportunities of praising the Disraelian Tory viewpoint and consequently condemning Gladstone and his politics. Gladstone is the 'Grand Old Mischief-maker';[9] he is soon 'the grand old traitor';[10] and 'Mr Gladstone ought to be beheaded on Tower Hill and buried in Westminster Abbey. . . . As I am accustomed to speak too strongly of him I will no further commit myself in writing.'[11] But Disraeli, 'of all eminent statesmen, was truly devoted to and truly promoted the honour of England; . . . he, a Jew born, was above all things a British patriot. That is the meaning of the primrose worship that goes on.'[12]

Hopkins was eminently sensible in his attitude towards both Ireland and India, as far as ever it was possible for a sensitive Tory to be. In a letter to Patmore, Hopkins says several interesting things regarding the British 'mission' in India and elsewhere: 'It is a terrible element of weakness that now we are not well provided with the name and ideal which would recommend and justify our Empire. "Freedom": it is perfectly true that British freedom is the best, the only successful freedom, but that is because, with whatever drawbacks, those who have developed that freedom have done so with the aid of law and obedience to law. The cry then should be Law and Freedom, Freedom and Law . . . our Empire is less and less Christian as it grows. . . . The best is gone, still something worth having is left. How far can the civilization England offers be attractive and valuable and be offered and insisted on as an attraction and a thing of value to India for instance? . . .'[13] Hopkins's views on Ireland and the Irish agitation for independence are dis-

---

[9] *Letters*, I, p. 257.   [10] ibid., p. 300.
[11] *Letters*, III, p. 110.   [12] ibid., p. 195.
[13] ibid., pp. 218-19.

tinguished by his human as well as typically Tory sympathies: 'Home Rule or separation is near. Let them come: anything is better than the attempt to rule a people who own no principle of civil obedience at all, not only to the existing government but to none at all. I shd. be glad to see Ireland happy, even though it involved the fall of England, if that could come about without shame and guilt. But Ireland will not be happy: a people without a principle of allegiance cannot be. . . . Something like what happened in the last century between '82 and 1800 will happen in this: now as then one class has passed off its class-interests as the interests of the nation and so got itself upheld by the support of the nation; now as then it will legislate in its own interest and the rest will languish; distress will bring on some fresh convulsion; beyond that I cannot guess.'[14] Hopkins sometimes writes with violence (the remarks on Gladstone can hardly have more of it); he has, in so far as he is a political animal, prejudices; but what really redeems these expressions of his political opinions is their commendable sincerity that painstakingly tries to see both sides to a question and is ultimately grounded in his fundamental humanity and charity.

Above all, Hopkins was a man of peace though he was also an Empire man, believing in an Empire whose bonds are forged on the anvil of justice and law and freedom. The beautiful and moving poem entitled 'Peace' is a surprisingly 'modernist' piece; but Christ himself was a man of peace, and no wonder his votary hymned the efficacy of Peace in a manner most ineffable—

When will you ever, Peace, wild wooddove, shy
                                            wings shut,
Your round me roaming end, and under be my boughs?

[14] *Letters*, I, p. 252.

When, when, Peace, will you, Peace? I'll not
                              play hypocrite
To own my heart: I yield you do come sometimes: but
That piecemeal peace is poor peace. What pure
                              peace allows
Alarms of wars, the daunting wars, the death of it?

O surely, reaving Peace, my Lord should leave in lieu
Some good! And so he does leave Patience exquisite,
That plumes to Peace thereafter. And when Peace
                              here does house
He comes with work to do, he does not come to coo,
  He comes to brood and sit.[15]

Here Hopkins the individual is yearning for peace, the peace that knows no qualification and is assigned no terminus; but the poem is no less humanity's own prayer for peace among the nations and lasting goodwill on earth.[16]

---

[15] *Poems*, No. 22.
[16] cf. Pick, p. 96: 'He (Hopkins) may have prayed for peace in a scrupulous concern for his own imperfections. For one who had so resolutely such a lofty concept of spiritual perfection, the path must have been steep. The sensitivity of his own failure to root out every evil and to cultivate every virtue must have given him great anguish.'

XV. IRELAND: THE TERRIBLE SONNETS: LAST DAYS

IN 1884 Hopkins was appointed Professor of Greek in the Catholic University College, Dublin. 'It is a new departure or a new arrival and at all events a new abode', he wrote to 'dearest' Bridges:[1] 'I have a salary of £400 a year, but when I first contemplated the six examinations I have yearly to conduct, five of them running, and to the Matriculation there came up last year 750 candidates, I thought that Stephen's Green (the biggest square in Europe) paved with gold would not pay for it. It is an honour and an opening and has many bright sides, but at present it has also some dark ones. . . . I have more money to buy books than room to put them in. I have been warmly welcomed and most kindly treated.'

Ireland has been to several Englishmen, even to a poet like Edmund Spenser, the El Dorado of their ambitions and also the graveyard of their hopes. With Fr Hopkins it was different, perhaps; he might have preferred to live in the England he loved so much, or in North Wales 'the true Arcadia of wild beauty',[2] in those places and scenes that he had immortalized in the magical spices of words and embalmed and consecrated with a rapturous devotion. But duty called, Greek had to be taught in the Catholic University efficiently, and the brilliant Balliol scholar and Benjamin Jowett's pupil[3] was the very man. Hopkins soon proved a success at the University. He had that particular

---

[1] *Letters*, I, pp. 189-90.   [2] *Letters*, III, p. 222.
[3] Jowett had called Hopkins 'the Star of Balliol' and described him as one of the best Greek scholars that had studied under him.

combination of profound scholarship in the subject and a profound sympathy for the young that makes for abiding popularity in a teacher. Besides, Fr Hopkins was odd; some even might have thought him mad in a way that was most winning. Did he not ask a cartman to drive eastward, and when the cart actually moved westward, fail to notice the difference? Had he not gleefully demonstrated the incident of Hector being dragged along by Achilles by pulling by the heels one of his own astonished pupils to and fro in the lecture hall? A Jesuit is an accomplished actor; the present writer remembers the vivid gesticulations and tonal modulations with which one of his Jesuit professors so successfully expounded *Othello*; he remembers too how another Jesuit Father, in such a dry subject as Astronomy, managed to galvanize with oscillations of his huge body, the quick movements of his hands and his sharp guttural sounds the queer happenings in our mysterious universe. With the histrionic sense in him so sharply developed, as it is in most Jesuits, and too, with a certain oddity in his temperamental composition, it was not strange that Fr Hopkins once sprang up in agitation as the plate of tarts arrived and cried in childish joy: 'Tartlets! Tartlets! My kingdom for a tart, Bernard, I love you!' It is also said that at another time Hopkins persuaded a common ploughman (perhaps it was Harry Ploughman) to teach him the so delectable art of ploughing.[4] To judge by appearances, then, Hopkins must have been very happy in Ireland.

But the fact remains that Hopkins was not happy, happy with the happiness earth understands. On 24 March 1885, he wrote to Bridges that he was 'weak in body and harassed in mind.'[5] Two months later he confessed to the

[4] Sargent, *Four Independents*, pp. 167-8.
[5] *Letters*, I, p. 211.

same correspondent: 'I think that my fits of sadness, though they do not affect my judgement, resemble madness.'[6] A few months later, again, he promised to send some sonnets to Bridges, five or more in number: 'Four of these', he further explained, 'came like inspirations unbidden and against my will. And in the life I lead now, which is one of a continually jaded and harassed mind, if in any leisure I try to do anything I make no way—nor with my work, alas! but so it must be.'[7] Later in the same letter Hopkins spoke with some passion about his futile attempts to write: 'If I could but get on, if I could but produce work I should not mind its being buried, silenced, and going no further; but it kills me to be time's eunuch and never to beget. After all, I do not despair, things might change, anything may be; only there is no great appearance of it.'

The sonnets that followed the letter, as we read and scrutinize them today, seem to strike a note of doubt, of despair even, not very unlike Job's outbursts. The sonnet-sequence, in its intensity of utterance, its naked revelation of a crucial spiritual insurrection, recalls some of Shakespeare's disturbing, lacerating, self-torturing sonnets, but is indeed more consistently and poignantly 'terrible'. In the first of the sonnets, 'Carrion Comfort', Hopkins agitatedly asseverates—

> Not, I'll not, carrion comfort, Despair, not feast
> on thee;[8]
> Not untwist—slack they may be—these last strands
> of man
> In me ór, most weary, cry *I can no more.* I can . . .

[6] *Letters*, I, p. 216.   [7] ibid., p. 221.
[8] cf. 'Thou oughtest not to be cast down, nor to despair ; but resign thyself calmly to the will of God, and whatever comes upon thee, to endure it for the glory of Jesus Christ.' (*The Imitation of Christ*).

Then come questions, complaints, incalculable arguments advanced against a strange 'adversary', all culminating in a terrifying recapitulation—

> But ah, but O thou terrible, why woudst thou rude on me
> Thy wring-world right foot rock? lay a lionlimb against me? scan
> With darksome devouring eyes my bruisèd bones? and fan,
> O in turns of tempest, me heaped there; me frantic to avoid thee and flee?
> Why? That my chaff might fly; my grain lie, sheer and clear.
> Nay in all that toil, that coil, since (seems) I kissed the rod,
> Hand rather, my heart lo! lapped strength, stole joy, would laugh, chéer.
> Cheer whom though? the hero whose heaven-handling flung me, fóot tród
> Me? or me that fought him? O which one? is it each one? That night, that year
> Of now done darkness I wretch lay wrestling with (my God!) my God.⁹

Was it of this sonnet that Hopkins wrote: 'If ever anything was written in blood one of these was'?¹⁰ Such a poem as this could only have been written in a moment of the most vivid ecstasy, not the ecstasy of joy, but of the most unbearable anguish. That one should be visited by pain, misery, one thousand heartaches, and, above all, by the crushing feeling of having proved Time's eunuch—that is no doubt a great pity; but there is an ecstasy too in the ordeal because one has had the nerve, the resignation and the strength of will to endure them all, to transmute them even into the pure gold of triumph! There is pleasure in the exquisiteness of a child's smile, and there is pleasure, of a severer

---

⁹ *Poems*, No. 40.   ¹⁰ *Letters*, I, p. 219.

kind, in the Thandav Dance of Shiva. Struggle and the mad whirl of action may issue in joy just as quiet and contentment sometimes lead to the peace that passeth understanding. With defeats, frustrations and multitudinous hurts man may be daunted, brought to bay; but if he dares all—never doubting though right were worsted wrong would triumph—he should feel the thrill of life's battle, and the thrill and the battle would be one and the same. Hopkins had the courage to dare and the faith to face the Hound of Heaven, to be mastered by it, to master himself. It was a terrible but purifying experience, a lacerating but life-giving emotion; and he has tried to render in memorable if disturbed accents this emotion and this experience.

The next sonnet arrests attention at once: 'No worst, there is none.'[11] Hopkins plies his 'enemy' with searching questions—

> Comforter, where, where is your comforting?
> Mary, mother of us, where is your relief? . . .

Then follow meditations, exhortations addressed to the poet's own self, expressions of anguished self-pity: and the sonnet concludes with a suggestion of the magnitude of the poet's trial and the pitiful ineptitude of the available remedies—also of the finality of the sole remedy, death—

> O the mind, mind has mountains; cliffs of fall
> Frightful, sheer, no-man-fathomed. Hold them cheap
> May who ne'er hung there. Nor does long our small
> Durance deal with that steep or deep. Here! creep,
> Wretch, under a comfort serves in a whirlwind: all
> Life death does end and each day dies with sleep.

Why, why should Hopkins, a Jesuit Father with hardly any worries, picture such desolation? Why should sonnets

---

[11] *Poems*, No. 41.

'complete in their gloom, awful in their anguish',[12] spirt out like 'inspirations' against one's will, by a sort of gravitational pull? 'All life death does end and each day dies with sleep.' Why should Hopkins assert this bleakness, this humiliating finale of the human tragedy? Is it the resignation of an unholy despair or the affirmation of a simple religious faith? Is it the reverse to the obverse of Shakespeare's, 'Death once dead there is no more dying then'?

The third sonnet seems to make a direct reference to his life in Ireland, and hence seems to state his personal problem fairly and squarely—

> To seem the stranger lies my lot, my life
> Among strangers . . .
> England, whose honour O all my heart woos, wife
> To my creating thought, would neither hear
> Me, were I pleading, plead nor do I: I weary of idle a being but by where wars are rife.
>
>   I am in Ireland now; now I am at a third
> Remove. Not but in all removes I can
> Kind love both give and get. Only what word
> Wisest my heart breeds dark heaven's baffling ban
> Bars or hell's spell thwarts. This to hoard unheard
> Heard unheeded, leaves me a lonely began.[13]

Hopkins is among strangers; he is a silent witness to nationalist Ireland's antipathy to England, and he is himself a typical Englishman, passionately fond of his own country. Why should England be so ruthless, Ireland so unbalanced? Why should the English be so unimaginative, the Irish so peevish and vindictive and indeed so silly? Hopkins was at the time writing to his friend Baillie: 'Home Rule of itself is a blow for England and will do no

---

[12] Herbert Read in 'The Poetry of Gerard Manley Hopkins' (*English Critical Essays, XXth century*, World's Classics, p. 358). [13] *Poems*, No. 44.

good to Ireland. But it is better than worse things. You would understand that if you lived in Ireland.'¹⁴ But one and all they were drifting—lazily, stupidly, suicidally drifting. And in the meanwhile, Fr Hopkins, S.J., soldier in the spiritual army founded by St Ignatius, was rusting unburnished though he was itching to shine in good use! His very thoughts, words, sanctified though they were in the sanctuary of his heart, were thwarted, set at naught, turned awry. And he must live and suffer in the stoniest silence! Such a poem as this can be said to bleed truly, dazing the beholders; the note of frustration, futility and disillusion sounds ominously throughout, as it were counterpointing the rhythm; and the picture of the 'lonely began' haunts our memories for ever.

The sonnet that follows is even more stark and unrelieved in its depictment of spiritual blight and misery—

I wake and feel the fell of dark, not day.
What hours, O what black hours we have spent
This night! what sights you, heart, saw; ways you went!
And more must, in yet longer light's delay.
  With witness I speak this. But where I say
Hours I mean years, mean life. And my lament
Is cries countless, cries like dead letters sent
To dearest him that lives alas! away.

  I am gall, I am heartburn. God's most deep decree
Bitter would have me taste: my taste was me;
Bones built in me, flesh filled, blood brimmed the curse.
  Selfyeast of spirit a dull dough sours. I see
The lost are like this, and their scourge to be
As I am mine, their sweating selves; but worse.¹⁵

This is a pulsing, piercing presentation of the mind in a state of frenzied despair. 'There is compression, but not beyond immediate comprehension; music, but a music of

¹⁴ *Letters*, III, p. 134.   ¹⁵ *Poems*, No. 45.

IRELAND: THE TERRIBLE SONNETS: LAST DAYS

overtones; rhythm, but a rhythm which explicates meaning and makes it more intense.'[16] Miss Babette Deutsch compares this sonnet with a well-known passage from Donne—

> Batter my heart, three person'd God: for, you
> As yet but knocke, breathe, shine, and seeke to mend;
> That I may rise, and stand, o'erthrow mee,'and bend
> Your force, to breake, blowe, burn and make me new . . .
> Yet dearly'I love you,'and would be loved faine,
> But am betroth'd unto your enemie:
> Divorce mee,'untie, or breake that knot againe,
> Take mee to you, imprison mee, for I
> Except you'enthrall mee, never shall be free,
> Nor ever chast, except you ravish mee.[17]

Miss Deutsch's comment is illuminating: 'There is the same violent conflict between the sceptical mind and the believing heart, the same anguished honesty and sensual alertness in the expression of the struggle, the same energy of feeling forcing the rhythm out of its natural smoothness, even the hard throb of the alliterative phrasing is the same.'[18] Just as in the earlier sonnet Hopkins suggested that the God he was wrestling with was 'his' God, his Friend who was also his Afflicter, he now affirms that it is 'by God's most deep decree' that he is tasting the bitterness of defeat. In the previous sonnet Hopkins wondered if 'dark heaven' or 'hell's spell' was thwarting him; now he has no doubts, he is surely in the hands of God, suffering or not suffering. The thunder clouds are looming large and are menacing, more than ever; sharp the hailstones hit, and batter down the defenceless body; but the clouds may break at any moment, a silver

---

[16] John Middleton Murry, *Aspects of Literature*, (Cape, Travellers' Library) p. 71.
[17] *Poems of John Donne*, ed. by Sir H. J. C. Grierson (Oxford University Press) p. 209.
[18] *This Modern Poetry*, p. 195.

lining however faint is visible already, and bright sunshine is not far off. But why should God, and Hopkins's own God, afflict him thus, shame him, shatter his self respect into splinters, shipwreck his innocent soul? It is amazing, inexplicable. But cannot Hopkins be a little more patient that His ordained purpose may be made manifest?

> Patience, hard thing! . . .
> . . . Natural heart's ivy, Patience masks
> Our ruins of wrecked past purpose. There she basks
> Purple eyes and seas of liquid leaves all day.
>
> We hear our hearts grate on themselves: it kills
> To bruise them dearer. Yet the rebellious wills
> Of us we do bid God bend to him even so.
> And where is he who more and more distils
> Delicious kindness?—He is patient. Patience fills
> His crisp combs, and that comes those ways we know.[19]

No, patience is no easy solution; it is a difficult and ruthless thing to practise, often a nerve racking experience; and, meanwhile, are there any other remedies? Can one forget —sink Lethe-wards, and drown present miseries for ever? Can one turn one's thoughts elsewhere, to other things, less cheerless, less crushing thoughts?

> Soul, self; come, poor Jackself, I do advise
> You, jaded, let be; call off thoughts awhile
> Elsewhere; leave comfort root-room; let joy size
> At God knows when to God knows what; whose smile
> 's not wrung, see you; unforeseen times rather—as skies
> Betweenpie mountains—lights a lovely mile.[20]

It is now apparent that Hopkins is getting accustomed to the whole fury of his spiritual disturbance and is prepared to live as best he may 'this tormented mind tormenting yet';

[19] *Poems*, No. 46.   [20] ibid., No. 47.

he is now willing, submissively and even hopefully, to bide his time. Not that this hope is very rational—for there are no signs that times are going to change, that Spring will follow in the wake of Winter—

> The times are nightfall, look, their light grows less;
> The times are winter, watch, a world undone:
> They waste, they wither worse . . .
> And I not help. Nor word now of success:
> All is from wreck, here, there, to rescue one—
> Work which to see scarce so much as begun
> Makes welcome death, does dear forgetfulness.[21]

And what is Man himself? Can he battle with his destiny, shape and mould it to his satisfaction? He is a negligible quantity—a speck of insignificance—in the the vast, inscrutable scheme of things in the universe. Man is no more than a 'scaffold of score brittle bones'; and 'hand to mouth he lives, and voids with shame'.[22] The prospect, seen every way, seems instinct with a pathetic inutility.

In perhaps the last sonnet of all, '*Justus quidem tu es, Domine*', Hopkins's tone is yet one of sadness, but this sadness is more severely restrained than in the earlier pieces; there is doubt, but it does not amount to despair; and there is an expression of prayerful hope not untinged with a vague certainty of ultimate fulfilment—

> Thou art indeed just, Lord, if I contend
> With thee; but, sir, so what I plead is just.
> Why do sinners' ways prosper? and why must
> Disappointment all I endeavour end?
>
>   Wert thou my enemy, O thou my friend,
> How woudst thou worse, I wonder, than thou dost
> Defeat, thwart me? Oh, the sots and thralls of lust
> Do in spare hours more thrive than I that spend,

[21] *Poems*, No. 60.   [22] ibid., No. 69.

> Sir, life upon thy cause . . .
> . . birds build—but not I build; no, but strain,
> Time's eunuch, and not breed one work that wakes.
> Mine, O thou lord of life, send my roots rain.[23]

The bareness, spareness of the phrasing, the pith of the agelong cry, heard in other climes, in other times, in Job, in Samson, in Harischandra, that evil triumphs and good is alas worsted, that the inferior are fruitful and multiply while the choice spirits wither and die, the heart-rending S.O.S. for the spiritual rain that should 'stir' the 'Waste Land' into fresh and fulsome life, the piercing pathos of the image of 'Time's eunuch', they all coalesce to make this sonnet hark back and forth to Shakespeare and Donne on the one hand and Eliot and Sri Aurobindo on the other. About the time this sonnet was written Hopkins was also writing to Bridges: 'Unhappily I cannot produce anything at all, not only the luxuries like poetry, but the duties almost of my position, its natural outcome—like scientific works. I am now writing a quasi-philosophical paper on the Greek Negatives: but when shall I finish it? or if finished will it pass the censors? or if it does will the *Classical Review* or any other magazine take it? All impulse fails me: I can give myself no sufficient reason for going on. Nothing comes: I am a eunuch—but it is for the kingdom of heaven's sake.'[24] The withering image of 'eunuch' again, for the third time in his works! But, in a sense, what Hopkins says is true. While Ireland is quite uncongenial

---

[23] *Poems*, No. 50. cf. Aldous Huxley: 'Never, I think, has the just man's complaint against the universe been put more forcibly, worded more tersely and fiercely than in Hopkins's Sonnet.' (*Texts and Pretexts*, Chatto & Windus, 1933, p. 67.)

[24] *Letters*, I, p. 270. 'And there are eunuchs, who have made themselves eunuchs for the kingdom of heaven.' (*St Matthew*.)

to literary activity, Hopkins finds that Wales is rather a
'mother of Muses' to him; while on a holiday there in
October 1886, he is able to give shape to a few scenes of his
projected play, *St Winefred's Well*;[25] he definitely hopes
to finish it,—but 'cannot say when'. But it could not be
completed—only a few fragments, though these are full of
promise and even contain individual passages of great
beauty and power, have come down to us. About the end
of 1886 Hopkins writes to Bridges that his book 'on the
Dorian Measure is going on, but may easily either wreck
(by external difficulties, examinations and other ones) or
founder (of its own).... Yet I hope, I do hope, to get out
something.'[26] Nothing finished comes out! Pathetically
Hopkins goes on, moaning the general, irreparable hurt his
system has somehow sustained: '... I do try to write at it;
but I see that I cannot get on, that I shall be even less able
hereafter than now. And of course if I cannot do what
even my appliances make best and easiest, far less can I
anything else. Still I could throw myself cheerfully into
my day's work? I cannot, I am in a prostration.'[27] So much
is Hopkins downcast at the thought of failure that even if a
finished article is rejected by the editor, he would be satisfied: 'to me, to finish a thing and that it shd. be out of hand
and owe its failure to somebody else is nearly the same thing
as success.'[28] He would be satisfied if he could do his part
of the work completely: but his attempts to get things done
are futile. 'For instance, I began an Epithalamion on my
brother's wedding: it had some bright lines, but *I could
not get it done*.' These six words seem to haunt the waking
and sleeping consciousness of Hopkins: he simply cannot
get away from the idea. 'Time's eunuch' he calls himself,

[25] *Letters*, I, p. 227. [26] ibid., pp. 246-7.
[27] ibid., p. 251. [28] ibid., p. 277.

again and again, in an agony of self-abasement; and this agony is excruciatingly sustained throughout the sonnet-sequence of the Irish period.

Reading such a profoundly moving sonnet-sequence as this we cannot help asking: Why, why ever did Hopkins feel the urge to write thus, almost as if his entire being quivered with a frenzy that insisted on expression in these uncompromising terms? Were there any reversals on the material plane that could have so moved Fr Hopkins? There were sorrows enough. He was weak and in failing health; he had to go through the tiresome routine of examining answer books. On 25 October 1884, he wrote to Canon Dixon: 'I have 557 papers on hand: let those who have been thro' the like say what that means.'[29] Many examiners in India go through as many papers and more, and are not much the worse for it; they reduce marking to a system (and the 'Moderators' help them to do so), and their hands move on with clock-like regularity, awarding passes and failures with practised unconcern. But Hopkins took this matter seriously; he weighed every answer in a critical balance and sat through scores and scores of hours discharging his duties conscientiously. The Irish scene, again, was not the congenial and stimulating thing North Wales had been, and rather damped his spirits and induced in him an unhealthy, intellectual in-breeding. Friends too he lacked, and he had therefore to content himself with receiving very occasionally a letter from Bridges or Dixon or Patmore. Of his colleague and companion in Dublin, Hopkins wrote to Bridges: 'My companion is not quite himself or he verges towards his duller self and so no doubt do I too, and we have met few people to be pleasant with.'[30] He aged perceptibly, he

[29] *Letters*, II, p. 123.
[30] *Letters*, I, p. 278.

withered: 'I am feeling very old and looking very wrinkled'. 'It seems to me,' he wrote again, 'I cannot always last like this: in mind or body or both I shall give way—and all I really need is a certain degree of relief and change; but I do not think that what I need I shall get in time to save me.'[31] It is true, then, that Hopkins suffered—but such suffering as this, worry over the assessing of examination papers, worry over one's health, cannot yet explain the acute misery and frenzy of desolation portrayed in the final sonnets. These latter seem to puzzle us owing to the inadequacy of words to express feelings unbearably poignant and individual in the extreme. The known inadequacies of Hopkins's life in Ireland are not so very unusual to have been the sole, or even the primary, cause of the spiritual nightmare so pointedly reflected in the sonnet-sequence. What then supplied the spiritual and emotional stimulus to these elaborations of pain, and doubt, and despair? Fr Lahey, a fellow Jesuit, attempts an explanation:

'Hopkins, smiling and joyful with his friends, was at the same time on the bleak heights of spiritual night with his God. All writers on mysticism—St Teresa, St John of the Cross, Poulain, Maumigny, etc.—have told us that this severe trial is the greatest and most cherished *gift* from One Who has accepted literally His servant's oblation. Hopkins was always remembered by all who met him as essentially a priest, a deep and prayerful religious. With the fine uncompromising courage of his initial conversion, he pursued his never-ending quest after spiritual perfection. The celebrated 'terrible' sonnets are only terrible in the same way that the beauty of Jesus Christ is terrible. Only the strong pinions of an eagle can realize the cherished happiness of such suffering. It is a place where Golgotha and Thabor meet. Read in this light his poems cease to be tragic.'[32]

[31] *Letters*, I, p. 282.
[32] Lahey, p. 143 ; also Underhill's *Mysticism* (Methuen, 1930) pp. 380-412.

The present writer is reminded of a Sanskrit verse that his grandfather often used to recite in which God assures, or warns, His devotees that He will inflict on them all possible sufferings, not in order to try their faith, but as a special favour! The struggle indicated in Hopkins's sonnets reminds us also of the content of some of the 'Holy Sonnets' of Donne; and especially the ninth is almost a precise anticipation of the last of Hopkins's sonnets—

> If poysonous mineralls, and if that tree,
> Whose fruit threw death on else immortall us,
> If lecherous goats, if serpents envious
> Cannot be damn'd; Alas; why should I bee?
> Why should intent or reason, borne in mee,
> Make sinnes, else equall, in mee more heinous?
> And mercy being easie, and glorious
> To God; in his stern wrath, why threatens hee?....[33]

Hopkins too, like Donne before him, like innumerable mystics before him, underwent the ordeal, gladly and on the whole gratefully; he knew it for a divine blessing, and he could prize it as such. But at odd, awful intervals, there came moments of perplexity and anguished seasons of devouring doubt. The faith that trusted and the doubt that questioned—the faith that looked upon rebuffs as part of the providential scheme and the doubt that dwelt sorely on the rebuffs and questioned why things were thus and thus and not otherwise—faith and doubt insistently wrangled, the whole solidity and compound mass of the ten-year religious training buttressing faith and the whole sinuous tenour of human sensibility reinforcing doubt; and out of this opposition of agreement and disagreement, this tension between

---

[33] *Poems of John Donne*, ed. by Sir H. J. C. Grierson, p. 297.

faith and doubt, was born the 'terrible' sonnet-sequence, terrible in its beauty and terrible too in its touching pathos.³⁴ The sonnets quiver with an almost unbearable poignancy because they rapturously strain after the union with God and the peace that passeth understanding—and they also moan that the union cannot be realized and the final peace cannot be achieved. That there was, for a short time, this feeling of failure, that there was this tension, this insurrection within the mind, is what concerns the student of poetry. But the stern faith of the true religious transcends the intimations, the self-torturings and the agonizing nightmares of the poet. The conflict between good and evil, form and disorder, is comprehended by the tragic poet in all its acuteness and apparent futility; and the ensuing poetry is profoundly moving—it finds an echo in our hearts. This vision, necessarily partial, has given us all the great tragic poetry that has gone to enrich the cultural heritage of the world. But an even keener vision beholds not merely the dichotomy but also the final achievement, not earth only but heaven also, and hymns boldly the praise of the ordainer of all order with unswerving and undying faith. We have no doubt at all that Hopkins attained this faith at last.

On 29 April 1889, Hopkins wrote to Bridges: 'I am ill to-day, but no matter for that as my spirits are good.'³⁵ He sent by the same letter a dedicatory sonnet as well, the

---

³⁴ Both Fr D'Arcy and Dr Pick think that the last sonnets have no connexion with mystic 'dark nights' but 'fall into what is well known as the season of dry and dark faith, a season during which most good people are deprived of all the old sensible delights they formerly enjoyed when thinking of God and all His saints. Faith is left without its natural supports and never wavers—and so prepares the way for a fuller dependence on God in hope and a greater union in charity.' (Pick, pp. ix-x.)   ³⁵ *Letters*, I, p. 303.

sestet of which is perhaps one of the most discerning pieces of self-criticism in the language—

> Sweet fire the sire of muse, my soul needs this;
> I want the one rapture of an inspiration.
> O then if in my lagging lines you miss
> The roll, the rise, the carol, the creation,
> My winter world, that scarcely breathes that bliss
> Now, yields you, with some sighs, our explanation.[36]

The last letter, the last poem Hopkins sent to his friend—and the poem itself dedicated to his friend! Was Fr Hopkins obscurely aware that his earthly travail was soon to be over? Soon after Easter Hopkins felt ill, seriously ill this time, and he was himself conscious of it. Early in June his condition became worse; the Holy Viaticum was administered to him; and it was clear he was a dying man. His parents came to see him; he had long ago been reconciled to them, and now he bade 'good-bye' to them and felt immeasurably happy; regrets, disappointments, bore no thinking at such a time; he was content simply to die, content to have striven towards perfection patiently, unflinchingly, to the last. He received the Holy Viaticum for the last time on the morning of 8 June 1889: 'the final blessing and absolution were also then given him at his own request, and he was heard two or three times to say "I am so happy, I am so happy". Soon afterwards, he became too weak to speak, but he appeared to follow mentally the prayers for the dying, which were said a little before noon by Fr Wheeler, and joined in by his parents. As the end approached he seemed to grow more collected, and retained consciousness almost up to the moment, half-past one o'clock, when he passed peacefully away. He was buried in

---

[36] *Poems*, No. 51.

the burial ground of the Society at Glasnevin,'[37] and his epitaph might have been, in his own words—

> ... Across my foundering deck shone
> A beacon, an eternal beam. Flesh fade, and mortal trash
> Fall to the residuary worm; world's wildfire,
>   leave but ash:
>   In a flash, at a trumpet crash,
> I am all at once what Christ is, since he was what
>   I am, and
> This Jack, joke, poor potsherd, patch, matchwood,
>   immortal diamond,
> Is immortal diamond.[38]

---

[37] Lahey, pp. 147-8.   [38] *Poems*, No. 48.

XVI. HOPKINS'S PROSODY

HOPKINS's has almost wholly been posthumous fame. Even as a Catholic he was obscure in his own lifetime; others, like Manning and Newman, also converts to Rome from the Anglican fold, impressed themselves indelibly on the intellectual and religious physiognomy of Victorian England. But Gerard Hopkins was a negligible quantity; he was known to a few intimate friends in England, to his pupils in the Dublin College: for the rest, he was practically nonexistent. Perhaps, had he lived to the ripe old age of either of the venerable Cardinals, he might have been able not only to render posterity a different and fuller account of his undoubted powers but also to gain recognition in his own lifetime for the work he accomplished. On the other hand, Hopkins the poet was doomed from the first in Victorian England. If the Jesuits' own magazine, *The Month*, dared not or did not care to publish 'The Wreck of the *Deutschland*' and 'The Loss of the *Eurydice*', what likelihood was there of his other poems, with their daring experiments in metre and rhyme, their unusual and outlandish vocabulary and their more or less pervasive obscurity, pleasing a public that had its taste fashioned in various ways by a Tennyson, a Swinburne, a Matthew Arnold, a Martin Tupper? As Thomas Lovell Beddoes, the author of *Death's Jest Book*, was saved for posterity by the loyal friendship of Thomas Kelsall, so to an even completer extent Gerard Manley Hopkins the poet was saved by the tender, if also conscientiously critical, friendship of a brother poet, Robert Bridges. And now Hopkins is hailed as a poet, an original poet, a poet's poet, terms that may be applied to him without reserve however their value may have been debased in our time by too much currency. The younger generation of poets, even the youngest colts in the lot, accept and revere and follow his leadership in several important respects. We shall now attempt to discuss the extent and nature of Hopkins's prosodical innovations, his experiments in rhyme, his alliterations and assonances, his extraordinary word-combinations and the validity or otherwise of his other technical devices.

English prosody is unfortunately a very confusing branch of study, and experts have made confusion worse confounded by their dogmatisms. Are we to follow the 'foot system' advocated, among others, by Professor Saintsbury? Or are we to discard it and follow the bar system in music which Lanier outlined and which has more recently been vehemently championed by Mr D. S. MacColl?[1] A line in verse consists of a number of words, and a word is made up of one or more syllables. Reading prose or verse is impossible if all the syllables are to be pronounced evenly; such a uniformity in speech is against the genius of the language itself. In a word like 'London' or 'Bookman', the stress is on the first syllable; we have only to try to put the stress on the second syllable to laugh at the absurdity of the thing. Monosyllabic words, especially words like 'on', 'in', 'a', 'the' and 'which', are ordinarily pronounced weakly; other words, monosyllabic or otherwise, may be stressed or not according to the exigencies of the sense. Thus when we read prose or verse, we automatically pronounce a few syllables strongly and the rest weakly, and these 'stressed' and 'unstressed' syllables more or less alternate; consequently, when we read

---

[1] 'Rhythm in English Verse, Prose, and Speech', *Essays and Studies by Members of the English Association*, Vol. V. (Oxford University Press, 1914).

aloud, there are crests and cusps in the resulting stream of sound, in fact there is 'rhythm'. The rhythm in prose, however, is very irregular; the distances between any two adjacent crests or cusps are not necessarily or even generally equal; there is a wavy motion, it is true, but the graph is not of the nature of a Sine or Cosine curve in Trigonometry. <u>Verse is distinguished from prose by this important criterion: rhythm in verse is much more regular than in prose.</u> If 'regular', regular in what sense, to what extent? Should each line in verse consist of a fixed number of syllables, these latter again grouped into various dumps or 'feet'? Should each line rather show its individuality by its 'stresses', a fixed number of them per line? Are the 'stresses' in a line of verse similar to 'bars' in music? These are controversial questions. Here is a line, the first in Hopkins's *Poems*—

I bēar a bāsket līned with grāss;

the line has eight syllables, and read naturally the 'stresses' fall on every even syllable. We may say that the line consists of four feet—(I bear), (a bas), (ket lined), (with grass)—each an *iambic* foot; we may say that the line consists of four *trochaic* feet—(bear a), (basket), (lined with), (grass * * *)—the last foot being completed by a silent syllable, or a 'rest'; we may even say that the line has four bars, corresponding to the four stresses, separated by equal quantities of time. However we consider the rhythm of this particular line, its regularity cannot be in question. The difficulty arises when we confront lines which are not so regular; it becomes necessary to formulate principles to justify the departures from the accepted norm of regular rhythm; and here prosodists vehemently disagree.

Let us consider two more lines from the same poem, 'For a Picture of St Dorothea'—

| Līlies I | shēw you, | līlies | nōne,* * *|
| Nōne in | Cāesar's | gārdens | blōw * * *|

The first line has four feet, of which the second and third are trochees, the first a dactyl (a stressed syllable followed by two unstressed ones) and the last a trochee though in the place of the unstressed syllable there is only a rest; the second line has clearly three trochaic feet, the fourth trochee, however, having a rest as in the previous line. We might describe these lines therefore as basically trochaic, 'lilies I' being a dactylic 'substitution' in the place of a trochee. In the same way in—

| But thēse | were fōund | in the Eāst | and Sōuth, |

there are obviously three iambic feet, the first, second and fourth; the third is an anapaest (a stressed syllable preceded by two unstressed ones) in the place of an iamb. Here we have an instance of an anapaestic substitution in the place of an iamb. Thus verse rhythm is regular in either being a succession of iambs or of trochees, in either case the distances between any two consecutive stresses in point of time being the same for the line; occasionally an anapaest is substituted for an iamb, or a dactyl for a trochee, but in such a manner that the stresses are not disturbed; in other words, the substituted anapaest (or dactyl) takes the same time for its utterance as the iamb (or trochee) would have taken had there been no substitution.

Here is yet another line from the same poem, 'For a Picture of St Dorothea', which is indeed full of experiments with stresses—

| Rāther | it īs | the sī|zing mōon.|

Here the movement is iambic, but the first foot, 'Rather', is a trochee: can a trochee, then, be substituted for an iamb? It is clear that the distance in time between the first and second stresses is longer than that between the second and third or the third and fourth. Does this destroy the regularity of the rhythm or 'metre'? Professor Saintsbury would consider such substitutions quite valid; the number of feet is the main thing, the disturbance in the time sequence of the stresses caused by a trochaic substitution in the place of an iamb does not matter at all. Similarly, an iamb in the place of a trochee, a dactyl in the place of an iamb or anapaest and in fact any foot in the place of any other kind of foot, are all valid. Mr D. S. MacColl, on the contrary, maintains that 'the musical law of rhythm alone can explain the structure of English verse'.[2] 'Metre', he writes more recently, 'is the regular measure of equal time-quantities marked by initial stress: rhythm includes an elastic play with those quantities which obtains expression not only by devices well known in music such as accelerando and ritardando, but by the extra-metrical use of "pauses", i.e. the dwelling on a note beyond its strict time-value'.[3] Mr MacColl would thus look upon verse as music pure and simple so far as scansion is concerned; accordingly, the foot-method of scansion advocated by the classical prosodists would not do. Naturally, therefore, Mr MacColl cannot agree that a trochaic substitution in the place of an iamb can ever be admissible: 'A metrical "foot" can no more be maltreated in this way than the human foot: the operation would be the equivalent of "reversing" under the ankle, the position of heel and toe. Nothing can alter the position of

---

[2] *Essays and Studies by Members of the English Association*, Vol. V, p. 8.
[3] *The London Mercury*, July 1938, p. 218.

the bar-stress: that is a fixed point round about which syllabic matter, with or without silences, adjusts itself.'[4] It is of the essence of English verse that it is 'a function of quantity and accent, the universal law being that equal quantities of time (called "bars" in music and hitherto "feet" in verse) are marked off by metrical accent.... When we listen to verse, even verse we have never heard before, we know exactly *when* the next accent must fall as surely as when we listen for the next stroke of a clock striking the hour, and if one accent is passed over in silence, we know exactly when the next again will fall, as surely as we do in the case when a stroke of the clock has been obscured by an interfering sound. We can do this only if there is a fixed relation of time between the accents.'[5] Mr MacColl's objections to the foot-system are not really as formidable as they seem. He allows that 'rests' or 'silences' are valid; when a trochee is substituted for an iamb, there is an unstressed syllable where a stressed should be, a flick in the place of a stroke. If a 'rest' can do duty for a stroke now and then, a flick can do that as well if not better; the preceding stroke is just 'an interfering sound' and need not destroy our sense of time. Provided, then, substitutions are not resorted to frequently, the ear will expect the strokes at the appropriate places, and will generally get them; an isolated trochee in the place of an iamb need not, and usually does not, cause a metrical disaster; on the contrary it produces the necessary variety. A line like Shakespeare's—

| Līe thĕre | my ārt, | wīpe thŏu | thĭne ēyes, | hăve cōm|fŏrt

[4] *The London Mercury*, July 1938, p. 223.
[5] *Essays and Studies by Members of the English Association*, Vol. V, pp. 27-8.

can only be considered to be an iambic line, with two trochaic substitutions (first and third); nevertheless its basic rhythm is not destroyed. It therefore appears that it is not impossible to reconcile the foot-system and the musical system, because that is exactly what the poets themselves seem to have done, however unconsciously. Verse, then, ceases to be regular, considered as a stream of sound, unless the strokes follow one another at regular intervals, occasional irregularities and silences being not ruled out; whether substitutions are valid or not, whether they really destroy the musical basis of verse or not, cannot be discussed *in vacuo*, but only with reference to the actual practice of the poets. Here as elsewhere nothing succeeds as success.

Hopkins seems to have tried to arrive at a compromise between the foot-system and the musical bar-system; but his own theory and practice are so unusual that they have scandalized the protagonists of both systems. We have seen already that Hopkins wrote 'The Wreck of the *Deutschland*' in a new rhythm that had long haunted his ears; he wrote many of his later poems also in the same rhythm. In his 'Preface', written probably in 1883, Hopkins elaborated his new theory of prosody; and this *tour de force* has now become almost as famous as Wordsworth's preface to his *Lyrical Ballads*. Hopkins finds in Common English Rhythm or Running Rhythm a succession of feet of either two or three syllables, 'never more or less'; each foot has a principal stress (or accent), the remaining syllable or syllables in the foot being 'slacks'; iambic and anapaestic feet constitute 'Rising' rhythm, while trochaic and dactylic feet constitute 'Falling' rhythm. 'These distinctions are real and true to nature; but for purposes of scanning it is a great convenience to follow the example of music and take the stress always first, as the accent or the chief accent always comes first in a musical bar.'⁶ If this were done there would be only two basic rhythms, the Dactylic and the Trochaic.

But since an orthodox succession of trochees (or of iambs or of any other kind of feet) will be monotonous like metronomical beats, all poets have, in greater or lesser measure, permitted themselves the liberty of occasionally substituting for the basic foot any of the three other kinds of feet, sometimes even the more unusual spondee, amphibrach, and so on. 'By a reversed foot I mean the putting the stress where, to judge by the rest of the measure, the slack should be and the slack where the stress, and this is done freely at the beginning of a line and, in the course of a line, after a pause; only scarcely ever in the second foot or place and never in the last, unless when the poet designs some extraordinary effect; for these places are characteristic and sensitive and cannot well be touched.'⁷ Almost all poets have done this, Shakespeare especially in his later plays.

Hopkins, however, thought that further freedom in versification was possible. First, Counterpoint: if, for instance, normally iambic verse is interpolated with frequent trochaic substitutions, 'especially so as to include the sensitive second foot', two rhythms may be said to co-exist, the basic iambic rhythm and the superimposed trochaic rhythm, and this conjunction of rhythms Hopkins called Counterpointed Rhythm. According to Hopkins the Choruses in Milton's *Samson Agonistes* are written through-

---

⁶ *Poems*, pp. 1-2.
⁷ ibid., p. 2. cf. Sri Aurobindo: '. . . . The rhythm can be varied or modulated by departures from the base—from it but always upon it; for these departures, variations or modulations, relieve its regularity which might otherwise become monotonous, but do not replace or frustrate the essential rhythm.' (*On Quantitative Metre*.)

out in Counterpointed Rhythm. Several such lines can no doubt be found in the Choruses—

Let us not break in upon him....

That heroic, that renowned....

Or the sphere of fortune raises....

These are trochaic lines, though the basic metre is iambic; but Hopkins judiciously adds that, in regard to these Choruses, Milton 'does not let the reader know what the ground-rhythm is meant to be and so they have struck most readers as merely irregular'.[8] Early examples of Counterpointed Rhythm in Hopkins are found in 'God's Grandeur' and 'The Starlight Night'—

And āll | is sēared | with trāde; | blēared, smeared | with tōil;
And wēars | mān's smudge | and shāres | mān's smell: | the
  sōil....

The grēy | lāwns cold | where gōld, | where quīck|gōld lies!
Wīnd-beat | whītebeam! | aīry a|bēles set | on a flāre!
Flāke-doves | sent flōat|ing fōrth | at a fārm|yard scāre!—
Ah wēll! | it is āll | a pūr|chase, āll | is a prīze....

Such verse with its unexpected turns and heights and shallows, when handled delicately and with artistic restraint, is an excellent instrument to ring changes with dexterity. But as Mr G. M. Young has wisely remarked, 'the fundamental, guiding principle in English poetry has always been: you must counterpoint to avoid monotony, but you must not silence the pattern. You can only work within limits, and if you go beyond them the result is prose.'[9]

But even the wide enough latitude of Counterpointed Rhythm did not satisfy Hopkins; he therefore resuscitated the

[8] *Poems*, p. 3.
[9] *The London Mercury*, December 1936, p. 120.

pre-Chaucerian English rhythm and christened it Sprung Rhythm. There are to be four kinds of feet, consisting of one, two, three and four syllables respectively; but the stress should fall on the first or the only syllable; and, besides, the four kinds of feet may be freely mixed so that any one may follow any other kind of feet. Hopkins claimed for Sprung Rhythm twice the flexibility of foot in the common Running Rhythm because in the former 'any two stresses may either follow one another running or be divided by one, two, or three slack syllables. But strict Sprung Rhythm cannot be counterpointed. In Sprung Rhythm . . . . the feet are assumed to be equally long or strong and their seeming inequality is made up by pause or stressing.'[10] Hopkins has used the word 'Sprung' in the sense of 'abrupt', and hence the term applies by rights 'only where one stress follows another running, without syllable between'.[11] Moreover, 'it is natural in Sprung Rhythm for the lines to be *rove over*, that is for the scanning of each line immediately to take up that of the one before . . . . and in fact the scanning runs on without break from the beginning, say, of a stanza to the end and all the stanza is one long strain, though written in lines asunder.'[12]

Hopkins does not pretend to have discovered or invented Sprung Rhythm. 'Ding, dong, bell' consists of three stressed syllables, and its rhythm is therefore 'sprung'; so is the rhythm of Tennyson's 'Break, break, break'. In Milton's *Samson Agonistes* there are lines like—

Thīs, | thīs is | hē; | sōftly a|whīle . . . .

Ō | mīrror of | ōur | fīckle | stāte . . . .

Īt is not | vīrtue, | wīsdom, | vālour | wīt, |
Strēngth, | cōmeliness of | shāpe, or | āmplest | mērit. . . .

[10] *Poems*, p. 4.   [11] *Letters*, II, p. 23.   [12] *Poems*, p. 4.

which seem to be written in Sprung Rhythm. Hopkins gives various other examples from Shakespeare, Campbell and Milton, and claims that 'what I do in the *Deutschland* etc. is to enfranchise them as a regular and permanent principle of scansion.'[13]

Just as Hopkins recognized four kinds of feet in every one of which the stress falls on the first or only syllable, he recognized four other kinds of feet in every one of which the stress falls on the last or the only syllable; these two sets of feet are appropriate respectively to *falling* and *rising* rhythms. Thus in the former, monosyllables, trochees, dactyls and first paeons will follow one another in any order they please; in rising rhythm, similarly, monosyllables, iambs, anapaests, and fourth paeons will follow one another in all sorts of permutations.[14] But Hopkins would prefer to 'recognize, in scanning this new rhythm, only one movement, either the rising .... or the falling .... and always keep to that'. Hopkins himself seemed, in his own practice, to show a decided preference for the falling rhythm, in which every foot begins with a stress like a bar in music.

Practically the whole of 'The Wreck of the *Deutschland*' and 'The Loss of the *Eurydice*' is written in Sprung Rhythm, and can be scanned only as such. Here are a few lines from the *Deutschland*—

| Hōpe had | grōwn grey | hāirs, |
| Hōpe had | mōurning | ōn,
| Trēnched with | tēars, | cārved with | cāres, |
| Hōpe was | twēlve hours | gōne ....

---

[13] *Letters*, I, pp. 44-6. cf. Whitman:
  'Cōme, | lōvely and | sōothing | dēath ....
  Lōst in the | lōving flōating ōcean of thēe,
  Lāved in the flōod of thy blīss, O dēath.'
[14] *Letters*, II, pp. 39-40.

> | Jōy | fāll to | thēe, fàther | Frāncis, |
> | Drāwn to the | Līfe that | dīed;
> With the | gnārls of the | nāils in | thēe, | nīche
>   of the | lānce, his
> | Lōvescape | crūcifīed . . . .

'Tears', 'carved'; 'joy', 'fall'; 'thee', 'niche'; these are pairs of stresses which no slack syllables separate. 'The May Magnificat' is another specimen of a poem written in Sprung Rhythm; here there are only four stresses in each of the first two lines and three in the third and fourth lines—

> Māy is Māry's mōnth, and Ī
> Mūse at that and wōnder why:
>   Her fēasts fōllow reason,
>   Dated due to season—
>
> Candlemās, Lādy Day;
> But the Lady Mōnth, Māy . . . .[15]

There are Sprung rhythms also in 'At the Wedding March'

>   Dēep, dēeper than divined . . . .
>
>   Dēals trīumph and immortal years . . . .[16]

A more complicated specimen is 'Spelt from Sibyl's Leaves':[17] in this unusually long sonnet there are several examples of one stress following another immediately, producing the startling abruptness typical of Sprung Rhythm—'tīme's vāst'; 'fīre-featuring'; 'pāshed—quīte'; 'whēlms, whēlms, ānd'; 'Oūr ēvening'—and so on. The long lines, with their subtle alliterative effects and complicated rhythmic motion, acquire the character of an incantation. One has first to learn to read it, following Hopkins's marking of the most important accents, remembering too that the sonnet is a musical

---

[15] *Poems*, No. 18.   [16] ibid., No. 28.   [17] ibid., No. 32.

elaboration to be heard and not to be read silently on the printed page; but once one has got into the spirit of the poem and has learned to read it expressively, it readily yields its beauty and harmony. It was of this sonnet probably that Hopkins wrote to Bridges: 'It is, as living art should be, made for performance ... its performance is not reading with the eye but loud, leisurely, poetical (not rhetorical) recitation, with long rests, long dwells on the rhyme and other marked syllables, and so on. This sonnet should be almost sung: it is most carefully timed in *tempo rubato*.'[18] Elsewhere Hopkins expatiated likewise on the peculiar merits of Sprung Rhythm: 'Why do I employ sprung rhythm at all? Because it is the nearest to the rhythm of prose, that is the native and natural rhythm of speech, the least forced, the most rhetorical and emphatic of all possible rhythms, combining, as it seems to me, opposite and, one wd. have thought, incompatible excellences, markedness of rhythm—that is rhythm's self—and naturalness of expression—for why, if it is forcible in prose to say 'lashed: rod', am I obliged to weaken this in verse, which ought to be stronger, not weaker, into 'lāshed birch-rōd' or something? My verse is less to be read than heard....'[19]

By far the most outstanding specimen of sustained Sprung Rhythm in Hopkins's practice is to be found in 'The Loss of the *Eurydice*'.[20] Hopkins warns us that in this poem 'the scanning runs on without break to the end of the stanza, so that each stanza is rather one long line rhymed in passage than four lines with rhymes at the ends.'[21] These are the opening stanzas—

> The Eurydice—it concērned thēe, O Lōrd:
> Thrēe hundred sōuls, O alās! on bōard,

[18] *Letters*, I, p. 246.
[19] ibid., p. 46.
[20] *Poems*, No. 17.
[21] ibid., p. 107.

Some aslēep unawākened, āll unwārned, elēven fāthoms fāllen

Where shē fōundered! Ōne strōke
Fēlled and fūrled them, the hēarts of oāk!
And flōckbells ōff the aērial
Dōwns' fōrefalls bēat to the būrial.

The third line of each stanza has three beats, the other lines four; but the number of unstressed syllables or slacks between two stresses varies from none at all in 'Dōwns' fōrefalls' to four in the first line above. Here is another vivid stanza—

| Tōo proud, | tōo proud, what a | prēss she | bōre!
| Rōyal, and | āll her | rōyals | wōre.
   | Shārp with her, | shōrten | sāil!
| Tōo late; | lōst; | gōne with the | gāle.

In the first line the four feet respectively are 'Too proud', 'too proud, what a', 'press she', 'bore'—and whatever the number of syllables in a foot, the stress falls invariably on the first. In the last line, again, 'lōst; gōne' are both stressed; there are two feet of one stressed syllable each only, one with two syllables, and one with three. Read suggestively, the stanza does arrestingly evoke the very action it describes. Indeed, the whole poem, distantly paralleled by Shelley's 'Skylark', is one swift, clear jet of penetrating melody, with the natural fading out in—

Not that hell knows redeeming,
But for souls sunk in seeming
   Fresh, till doomfire burn all,
Prayer shall fetch pity eternal.

Of course, the internal assonances and alliterations are partly responsible for making Sprung Rhythm a success in this as also in Hopkins's other triumphant pieces. For, as Mr Megroz correctly points out, 'the strong alliterations and the rhyming upon unwonted words or syllables are necessary adjuncts of sprung rhythm. The alliterative emphasis is an important factor in keeping the mind suspended over intervening syllables until it reaches the stress which marks another foot. Follows also a great increase in grammatical inversions, and extraordinarily long phrases consisting of a sequence of nouns or adjectives.'[22] But the more Hopkins is at pains to produce his sound effects, the more it becomes imperative on the part of the reader to read the poem suggestively aloud before attempting to criticize its rhythm. This point Hopkins was never tired of making: 'To do the *Eurydice* any kind of justice you must not slovenly read it with the eyes but with your ears, as if the paper were declaiming at you. For instance the line "she had cōme from a crūise trāining sēamen" read without stress and declaim is mere Lloyd's Shipping Intelligence; properly read it is quite a different thing.'[23] Again: 'When, on somebody returning me the *Eurydice*, I opened and read some lines, reading, as one commonly reads whether prose or verse, with the eyes, so to say, only, it struck me aghast with a kind of raw nakedness and unmitigated violence I was unprepared for: but take breath and read it with the ears, as I always wish to be read, and my verse becomes all right.'[24] In other words, Hopkins, like D. H. Lawrence, hated a military on-foot method of reading poetry; he would have us read rather with all our senses alert, and the understanding as well.

It is needless to point out what incomparable freedom

---

[22] R. L. Megroz, *Modern English Poetry* (Ivor Nicholson and Watson, 1933), p. 237.
[23] *Letters*, I, pp. 51-2.   [24] ibid., p. 79.

the adoption of Sprung Rhythm gives to the practitioner of verse, especially since, according to Hopkins, two licenses are natural to it: 'the one is rests, as in music; . . . the other is *hangers* or *outrides*, that is one, two, or three slack syllables added to a foot and not counting in the nominal scanning.'[25] An example of the first type of license is in 'The Leaden Echo and the Golden Echo'—

> How to kéep—is there ány any, is there none such, nowhere known some, bow or brooch or braid or brace, láce, latch or catch or key to keep
> Back beauty, keep it, beauty, beauty, beauty, . . . from vanishing away?[26]

There is a rest at the place indicated by the three dots; another example is this from 'Spelt from Sibyl's Leaves'—

> Earnest, earthless, equal, attuneable, vaulty, voluminous, . . . stupendous
> Evening strains to be tíme's vást, womb-of-all, home-of-all, hearse-of-all night.

Here the rest is after 'voluminous'. Examples of the second type of license, outrides, are ample in Hopkins's poetry. For example in the fourth line of every stanza of 'The Bugler's First Communion',[27] there are superfluous syllables between the third and fourth feet—

> Low-latched in leaf-light housel his too huge
>   godhead . . .
>
> Breathing bloom of a chastity in mansex fine . . .

Other successful examples are found in 'Felix Randal', 'Hurrahing in Harvest', 'That Nature is a Heraclitean Fire' and in one or two other poems; the following is from 'Felix

[25] *Poems*, pp. 4-5.   [26] ibid., No. 36.   [27] ibid., No. 23.

Randal'[28] in which the outriding syllables at the end of the lines take the poem 'through many a winding bout of linked sweetness long drawn out'—

> How far from then forethought of, all thy more
> boisterous years,
> When thou at the random grim forge, powerful
> amidst peers,
> Didst fettle for the great grey drayhorse his bright
> and battering sandal!

Sprung Rhythm, with its attendant liberties of roving over, rests and outrides, is thus an instrument of tremendous efficacy in the hands of an adept. A line of, say, five feet, may have anything from five syllables (if with rests, an even fewer number) to twenty (if with outrides, an even greater number); and two stresses may either come together (one as it were springing on another), or be separated by three or, if with outrides, by as many as six syllables! Besides, as we have seen already, Hopkins claimed for Sprung Rhythm historical sanction as well. It is the rhythm of common speech and rhythmic prose, of nursery rhymes and weather saws; it was used by Langland in his *Piers Plowman*; it was used in Latin and Greek lyrics; it was used fitfully by Greene; 'it existed in full force in Anglo-Saxon verse and in great beauty';[29] and 'it is the rhythm of all but the most monotonously regular music, so that in the words of choruses and refrains and in songs written closely to music it arises.'[30] Mr Herbert Read goes further in his emphasis on the historical validity of Sprung Rhythm: 'The whole tradition of Teutonic and Norse poetry favours the principle of sprung rhythm. So that we may say that the tradition of sprung rhythm to which Hopkins returned

---

[28] *Poems*, No. 29. [29] *Letters*, I, p. 156.
[30] *Poems*, p. 5.

has a tradition within our own linguistic world at least twice as long as the tradition of running rhythm. For running rhythm was only established in England in the sixteenth century, whereas sprung rhythm had existed for at least eight centuries before that time.'[31] Anglo-Saxon prosody revolved round the twin principles of alliteration and stress; on these two also Hopkins has built up his own prosodic scheme. A forceful and elastic rhythm and innumerable linguistic devices are made to fuse into such art that it 'makes the verse sparkle like rich irregular crystals in the gleaming flow of the poet's limpid thought.'[32]

On the other hand, the torchbearers of tradition point out that in the undoubted elasticity of Sprung Rhythm lies also its danger, its basic weakness. While Sprung Rhythm, when wielded by a master like Hopkins (and not always even then), may be effective enough with its complicated attack and musical elaboration, it may degenerate in inept hands into cacophonous and gruff tomfoolery. Hopkins himself felt the need in several places to indicate his stresses—and these now and then seem forced, occasionally very unnatural, and yet they have to be so stressed for purposes of scansion. Is Hopkins writing, one occasionally asks oneself, to justify and illustrate his theory, or is his theory merely a generalization of his own and other people's practice? 'The Wreck of the *Deutschland*', 'The Loss of the *Eurydice*', 'Hurrahing in Harvest' and his other great triumphs do not owe their success to their rhythm, but rather to the emotion sustaining them. What, after all, do Hopkins's prosodical theories amount to? Firstly, that stresses are, like bars in music, the ordainers of rhythm; secondly, feet are made up of either a solitary stress or of a

---

[31] *English Critical Essays*, (XXth century), p. 366.
[32] Read, ibid., p. 368.

stress and one to three slacks, these either preceding the stress in a lump or in like manner following it; thirdly, the feet are equally long and strong, and hence stresses are separated from one another by equal intervals of time. If poetry can be written strictly in accordance with these principles, such poetry should be distinguished by both variety and a musical quality. But, in practice, it is difficult to linger over monosyllabic feet too long or hurry over tetrasyllabic feet too much without at the same time palpably making the reading ridiculous. Occasionally such modulations in voice may really enhance the significance of a passage but not always; in any case a passage in Sprung Rhythm cannot be read at the first instance as satisfactorily as can a passage in running rhythm. 'The Windhover', 'The Leaden Echo and the Golden Echo', 'Spelt from Sibyl's Leaves' and 'That Nature is a Heraclitean Fire' are some of the poems that baffle one in many places when one tries to read them for the first time. But when they are read again and again (just as a song is practised again and again), one gradually masters their rhythmic intricacies, the stresses fall in their appointed places, and the whole theme is galvanized into a stream of sound that keeps one's faculties fully engaged. Hopkins's theories of prosody are not very different from Mr MacColl's; like Mr MacColl's, Hopkins's too is a substantially musical notation; and, again like Mr MacColl, Hopkins too sees little difference between rhythmic prose and verse.[33]

If Sprung Rhythm as used by Hopkins is a thing of as much variety and complexity as a piece of music, to be

---

[33] In an article in *Life and Letters Today*, June 1939, Glyn Jones seeks to prove Hopkins's indebtedness to the Welsh *cynghanedd*, 'a combination of alliteration and internal rhyme regulated into a system of great strictness and intricacy'. But the argument does not sound quite convincing.

mastered only by those who are willing to take the necessary pains over the matter, it is clear that poetry written in this rhythm will deprive the average reader of one of his choicest pleasures—that of participating in the rhythm and anticipating its movement accurately from the first. When Milton's 'L'Allegro', for instance, is read, even for the first time, one can respond immediately to its swing, its regular rhythm. Stress and slack alternate so precisely that one can imagine oneself actually participating in the composition of such verse as—

> Haste thee, nymph, and bring with thee
> Jest and youthful Jollity,
> Quips and Cranks, and wanton Wiles,
> Nods, and Becks, and Wreathèd Smiles....

As we read such verses written in the traditional running rhythm, iambic or otherwise, our vocal organs are attuned to the measure, and we respond to the alternation of stresses and slacks without the slightest puzzlement; but with Sprung Rhythm we may be deceived any moment and we must be as wary as if we are reading prose, more wary perhaps! Sprung Rhythm at once makes verse as incalculable as prose and also, at its most successful, as intricate a fabric of sound as music. Running rhythm ordinarily is too formal and too mechanical and too unnatural; again, it is incapable of complicated musical effects. Sprung Rhythm as illustrated in a poem like 'Hurrahing in Harvest' or 'Felix Randal' does achieve the masculine directness and force of effective prose as also the disturbing exquisiteness and magic of entrancing music.

Sprung Rhythm in itself is thus fraught with very real dangers; if freely and unintelligently employed, the reader will lose the pleasure of immediately responding to the rhythm but will gain no counterbalancing advantages; in the end verse will be merely prose run mad. Hopkins phenomenally succeeded with Sprung Rhythm because the words he used were invariably charged with poetic significance, and, besides, phonetically he knit words into a wonderful scheme of intriguing and unescapable beauty. One would not certainly wish Hopkins's poems to be other than what they are; they may puzzle and tantalize us at first; booby traps may frighten us every now and then; oddities and crudities in expression may scare the conventionally sensitive reader away; but read with an honest intellectual effort, with one's whole being in attention, the mazes all clear away, the stresses fall in their proper places, and we are at last able to participate in the seething urgency of the poems and their spiritual content and rhythmic motion. It is not much use pontifically legislating what is permissible to the poet and what is not. Even Mr G. M. Young, who is decidedly against modern prosodical innovations, is prepared to acknowledge his 'great admiration' for Hopkins as a poet.[34] Had Hopkins merely borrowed the elements of stress prosody from Langland and the Anglo-Saxon poets, his Sprung Rhythm might have become indistinguishable from free verse or poetic prose. But Hopkins took over as well, and embellished besides, the energetic and nervous alliteration, the heavy on-rush of sheer verbal music, the 'thematic invention' (in Mr Ezra Pound's suggestive phrase), and the vivid and picturesquely evocative vocabulary characteristic of Old and most Middle English verse. The 'elements' were indeed all there, but Hopkins mixed them uniquely in the crucible of his imagination and Sprung Rhythm emerged at last as a valid principle of verse mechanics from the imponderable symphonies of 'The Wreck of the *Deutschland*'. Since then this fascinating

[34] *The London Mercury*, December 1936, p. 120.

measure has lured many a practitioner of verse and has served as a model to several of the poets of yesterday and today. However orthodox prosodists may scoff at Sprung Rhythm, it has already amply justified itself, illustrating thereby the truth of J. K. Stephens's witty remark that genius—

> . . . finds out what it cannot do
> And then it goes and does it.

Of course, Sprung Rhythm constitutes no more than the mechanics of Hopkins's most characteristic poetry, which, as all great poetry must be, is *sui generis* and hence not to be blindly imitated. As a writer pointed out in *The Times Literary Supplement* some time ago, 'There could be no better proof that real style is inimitable than the verse of those who have tried to play the sedulous ape to Hopkins. They have been few, and they have only succeeded in reflecting his mannerisms.'[35] On the other hand, it is idle to deny that Hopkins's prosodical theories and experiments have opened fascinating new horizons to our gaze. It is not unlikely that the present vogue for Sprung Rhythm will increase rather than decrease with time.[36]

---

[35] 26 September, 1942.
[36] cf. Herbert Read: '. . . before another generation has passed, I doubt if any other measure but sprung rhythm will be in use.' (*A Coat of Many Colours*, p. 160.)

XVII. TECHNICAL AND LINGUISTIC EXPERIMENTS

We have spoken at some length about Hopkins's prosody. A not less important feature of Hopkins's poetry and one that is integral to its constitution is his vigorous and compelling vocabulary. Hopkins's alliterative devices, of course, stare one in the face everywhere, and it is impossible to ignore them. Any line almost could be chosen at random, and it bristles with striking examples—

From life's *d*awn it is *d*rawn *d*own....

The *rec*urb and the *rec*overy of the gulf's sides....

In *c*risps of *c*url off *w*ild *w*inch *w*hirl, and *p*our
And *p*elt music, till none's to *sp*ill nor *sp*end....

*Qu*elled or *qu*enched in *lea*ves the *lea*ping sun....

*B*eauty's *b*earing or *m*use of *m*ounting vein....

Only the *b*eak-leaved *b*oughs *d*ragonish *d*amask the
tool-smooth *bl*eak-light; *bl*ack,
Ever so *bl*ack on it....

And so on. Sometimes the alliteration is associated with half-rhymes like 'heeds but hides', 'bodes but abides'; the consonants are identical, only the vowels are different. Several modernists (and even earlier poets) have tried to avoid rhyme as being the cause of considerable artificiality in poetic utterance. But rhyme, even like metre and alliteration, is firstly a means of restraining the undue effervescence of the poet's untrammelled utterance, and, secondly, of making poetic expression musical and memorable; great poets have worked within the restraints imposed by metre, rhyme and occasionally even alliteration, and have none the less written indubitable poetry. Hopkins had faith in rhyme and other similar devices used by English poets; and indeed rhymes are part of the genius of the English language. As Professor Basil de Selincourt remarks, 'Rhyme, in English poetry, reinforces accent, it helps to mark the distribution of the measure, it announces the conclusion of a verse. When two verses belong together, it is the link between them, the sign of their unity.'[1] To the extent Hopkins claimed freedom in versification by the formulation and adoption of Sprung Rhythm, to an equal, if not greater, extent he accepted the shackles of rhymes, assonances and alliterative devices of all sorts. His rhymes are not merely end-rhymes, but sometimes initial and sometimes interior rhymes; rhyming, then, is an extended and complex principle in his verse. We have interior rhymes like—

Was *around* them, *bound* them or *wound* them with her . . . .

Now he wrings for *breath* with the *death*gush brown . . . .

Is strung by *duty*, is strained to *beauty* . . . .

Let him *ride*, her *pride*, in his triumph . . . .

All the *air* things *wear* that build this world of Wales . . . .

In a passage like this we have initial, internal and end rhymes—

Christ *minds*; Christ's interest, what to avow or *amend*
There, eyes them, heart *wants*, *care haunts*, foot
                                       follows *kind*,
Their ransom, *their* rescue, and first, *fast*, *last* friend.

[1] *Essays and Studies by Members of the English Association*, Vol. VII, p. 10.

In Wilfred Owen also we have such rhymes; half-rhymes or para-rhymes (as Mr Edmund Blunden chooses to call them) are especially abundant in poems like 'From my Diary, July 1914'—

>   *Leaves*
>   *M*ur*m*ering by *m*yri*a*ds in the sh*imm*ering trees.
>   *Lives*
>   *W*aking *w*ith *w*onder in the Pyrennees.
>   *Birds*
>   *Ch*eerily *ch*irping in the early day.
>   *Bards*
>   *S*inging of *s*ummer *s*cything thro' the hay.

And so on; 'A mead .... a maid', 'Braiding .... brooding', 'Stirs .... stars' and other similar half-rhymes have acquired considerable currency today owing to their exploitation by Owen and Hopkins. But it is impossible to determine if or to what extent Owen himself was influenced by Hopkins.

Hopkins's alliterative devices are many and varied; unlike orthodox alliteration in grammar books, Hopkins's is a sinuous, pervasive thing, not restricted to the first letters only of the words, but coursing the entire gamut of sound and yielding an almost bewildering symphony. Not seldom Hopkins adds to the device of alliteration other artifices like repetition and assonance so that the whole may enrapture the attentive reader with its vibrant exquisiteness—

> Come then, your ways and airs and looks, locks, maiden gear,
>   gallantry and gaiety and grace,
> Winning ways, airs innocent, maiden manners, sweet looks,
>   loose locks, long locks, lovelocks, gaygear,
>   going gallant, girlgrace—
> Resign them, sign them, seal them, send them, motion
>   them with breath....[2]

---

[2] *Poems*, No. 36.

TECHNICAL AND LINGUISTIC EXPERIMENTS

Have fair fallen, O fair, fair have fallen, so dear
To me, so arch-especial a spirit as heaves in Henry Purcell
An age is now since passed, since parted....
The thunder-purple seabeach plumed purple-of-
thunder....[3]

Of the delicate threads with which Hopkins knit together such amazing webs of beauty and passion, Mr Charles Williams writes: 'First, they persuade us of the existence of a vital and surprising poetic energy; second, they suspend our attention from any rest until the whole thing, whatever it may be, is said.'[4] A poem like 'The Blessed Virgin compared to the Air we Breathe' is full of the subtlest similitudes in thought and feeling, and reading it one is constantly reminded of Donne and the other metaphysical poets of the seventeenth century—

> If I have understood,
> She holds high motherhood
> Towards all our ghostly good
> And plays in grace her part
> About man's beating heart,
> Laying, like air's fine flood,
> The deathdance in his blood;
> Yet no part but what will
> Be Christ our Saviour still.
> Of her flesh he took flesh:
> He does take fresh and fresh,
> Though much the mystery how,
> Not flesh but spirit now
> And makes, O marvellous!
> New Nazareths in us,
> Where she shall yet conceive
> Him, morning, noon, and eve;
> New Bethlems, and he born
> There, evening, noon, and morn—[5]

---

[3] *Poems*, No. 21.   [4] ibid., Introduction, p. xii.
[5] ibid., No. 37.

Air is the principle of physical life; and the Blessed Virgin and her Son constitute the principle of spiritual life, quietening and chastening our animal preoccupations, forging our kinship to the powers above. In such an extended simile as this it is Hopkins's religious ecstasy that bears the weight of the chains of similitudes and saves them from merely irritating the reader. On the contrary, emotion and conviction so inform the poem throughout that chanting it aloud one registers a series of intellectual surprises followed in the end by a spiritual calm that comes only from the profoundest poetical utterances.

Many of Hopkins's extraordinary combinations of words are flashes into the realm of meaning, iridescent thoughts, illuminations; music and meaning are jerked at us at once like thunder and lightning, and the tension of agreement in disagreement makes them assault us with a disturbing potency. Examples can be found on almost every page of Hopkins's poetry: 'fickle, freckled', 'down-dugged, ground-hugged', 'now burn, new born', 'wear man's smudge and share man's smell', 'bell-swarmed, lake-charmed', 'womb-of-all, home-of-all', 'blood-gush, blade-gash', 'wind-wandering, weed-winding', 'hoard unheard, heard unheeded', 'lush-kept, plush-capped', 'warm-laid grave of a womb-life grey', 'wind lifted, windlaced', 'wretches, on crutches', 'wind-beat whitebeam', and indeed their name is legion. Another way in which Hopkins has enriched our vocabulary is by joining existing words to form new words with new significances: 'heavengravel', 'wolfsnow', 'doomfire', 'fallowbootfellow', 'churlsgrace', 'Amansstrength', 'disseverel', 'selfyeast', 'lionlimb', 'seraph-arrival', 'leafmeal', 'shadow-tackle', and so on. Again, Hopkins's adjectives and picturesque descriptive phrases astonish and subdue us with their pertinent evocation of

TECHNICAL AND LINGUISTIC EXPERIMENTS 177

colour and gradual unfolding of the meaning: examples taken at random are 'circle-citadels', 'gash gold-vermilion', 'daregale skylark', 'dapple-with-damson west', 'crimson-cresseted east', 'mealed-with-yellow-sallows', 'dapple-dawn-drawn Falcon', 'world-wielding shoulder', 'dapple-eared lily', 'world-mothering air', 'forth-and-flaunting sun', 'all-a-leaf of the treetop' and 'hoar-hallowed shrines'. How much, indeed, Hopkins was preoccupied with the problem of giving the most figurative expression to his awareness of objective nature can be gauged from the following notes, in which the varied images by means of which he desired to fix the fugitive idea perfectly can be scrutinized together:

'Stars like gold tufts.
— — golden bees.
— — golden rowels.
Sky peak'd with tiny flames.
Stars like tiny-spoked wheels of fire.'[6]
'Reflection of stars in water.—Pointed golden
  drops. Gold tails.'[7]

Such explorations into the realms of nature and of language, such images turned out of the fiery forge of Hopkins's imagination, are at their best sheer emanations of thought, arrows accurately hitting the bull's eye. 'Gash-gold vermilion' or 'cast by conscience out' or 'stallion stalwart' or 'sinew service' is no elaborately artificial word-combination: 'Each is thought and spoken all at once; and this is largely (as it seems) the cause and (as it is) the effect of their alliteration. They are like words of which we remember the derivations; they present their unity and their elements at once.'[8]

Considering these achievements on the plane of language, one feels that Hopkins, like other great literary

[6] *Note-Books*, p. 32.   [7] ibid., p. 29.
[8] Williams, *Poems*, Introduction, pp. xi-xii.

geniuses, has a kind of sixth sense for the semantic and phonetic potentialities of words and combinations of words. This enabled him at times to pack questions, exclamations, parenthesis, generalization, description, all within a line or two:

> But how shall I . . . make me room there:
> Reach me a . . . Fancy, come faster—
> Strike you the sight of it? look at it loom there,
> Thing that she . . . there then! the Master
> *Ipse,* the only one, Christ, King, Head . . .[9]

> Buy then! bid then!—What?—Prayer, patience,
>   alms, vows.
> Look, look: a May-mess, like on orchard boughs!
> Look! March-bloom, like on mealed-with-yellow
>   sallows![10]

> A beetling baldbright cloud thorough England
> Riding: there did storms not mingle? and
> Hailropes hustle and grind their
> Heavengravel? wolfsnow, worlds of it, wind there?[11]

Sufficient has been said here to show that, even had Hopkins not been worthy of reverent study by virtue of the 'thought' in his poetry (but he is!), his experiments in stress prosody and his exploitation of the resources of language would alone entitle him to be considered one of the important poets in English literature.

It is now pertinent to refer to the many defects in style and idiom in Hopkins's poetry so carefully enumerated by the late Robert Bridges and also by other critics, both admirers and detractors of the poet's work. The charge of obscurity against Hopkins's poetry has already been glanced at. Hopkins himself was aware that his poetry was in places

---

[9] *Poems*, No. 4.   [10] ibid., No. 8.
[11] ibid., No. 17.

very obscure; but he always maintained that such obscurity as was there was inevitable. He wished to be read diligently, he wished that his readers would *think* when they read him; after supplying Bridges with a paraphrase of 'Tom's Garland', Hopkins exclaims, 'O, once explained, how clear it all is!'[12] He could not but compress his thoughts to breaking point in his poems—his whole training as a Jesuit made any other course impossible; he would, however, he proposed to Bridges, 'prefix short prose *arguments* to some of my pieces'.[13] He added further, by way of justification: 'Epic and drama and ballad and many, most, things should be at once intelligible; but everything need not and cannot be. Plainly if it is possible to express a subtle and recondite thought on a subtle and recondite subject in a subtle and recondite way and with great felicity and perfection, in the end, something must be sacrificed, with so trying a task, in the process, and this may be the being at once, nay perhaps even the being without explanation at all, intelligible. Neither, in the same light, does it seem to be to me a real objection . . . that the argument should be even longer than the piece; for the merit of the work may lie for one thing in its terseness.'[14] It may be, as Sir Arthur Quiller-Couch points out,[15] that the very greatest truths are really so simple that a child could be made to understand them; but all knowledge is not so simple, cannot be. Einstein's Theory of Relativity is a piece of important knowledge, but a child cannot understand it. Some of Hopkins's poems too cannot be comprehended on a casual reading; but they yield their meaning when studied with care, and hence their obscurity

---

[12] *Letters*, I, p. 273.   [13] ibid., p. 265.
[14] ibid., pp. 265-6.
[15] *Art of Reading* (Pocket Edition, Cambridge University Press), p. 61.

is only a temporary obstacle to our appreciating them.[16] Bridges has correctly pointed out that the main sources of obscurity in Hopkins's poetry are, first, the habitual omission of the relative pronoun ('because they took up room which he thought he could not afford them'), and, secondly, the grammatically ambiguous use of words.[17] 'What was the feast followed the night'; 'a lonely began'; 'mother have lost son'; 'O Hero savest'; 'it is the rehearsal of own, of abrupt self there so thrusts on, so throngs the ear'; such examples can easily be multiplied. In instances where Hopkins, aiming at compression and at the elimination of all unnecessary words, merely achieved obscurity, he proved a martyr to his theories and failed to establish communication with his reader, which, after all, should be the aim of every artist; but, fortunately, such excrescences are not very numerous in the body of Hopkins's work.

Objection has also to be taken to Hopkins's oddity and to the unorthodox and barbarous rhymes he has occasionally perpetrated. Hopkins the man was an odd creature; he was also an odd Jesuit; and inevitably his oddity is reflected in his poetry. His sonnets, for instance, rarely preserve the norm more or less standardized by the great English sonneteers. He believed that the English sonnet, in comparison with the Italian, is 'short, light, tripping, and trifling'.[18] And hence, to make his own sonnets approximate in spirit and length to the Italian, he weighted his lines with a vast burden of extra syllables and even of stresses so that sonnets like 'The Windhover', 'Spelt from

[16] cf. '... lucidity is not an absolute but a relative virtue —relative to the reader's sympathy and to the complexity and remoteness from ordinary experience of the thought or vision to be communicated.... A new secret may demand a new idiom, and we must have ears to hear it.' (Charles Morgan, *The Times Literary Supplement*, 3 July, 1943.)
[17] *Poems*, pp. 97-8.   [18] *Letters*, II, p. 86.

Sibyl's Leaves', 'Felix Randal', and 'Hurrahing in Harvest' look far more substantial poems than the sonnets of other English writers. On the other hand, the same Hopkins experimented on a shortened form of the sonnet as well, and gave it the name 'curtal sonnet'; 'Pied Beauty' and 'Peace' are his own exhibits of this type. Each of these curtal sonnets consists of ten lines and a half; and this number is arrived at by taking three fourths of the octave and sestet respectively of the normal sonnet, in other words six lines and four and a half lines. The itch for innovation that made Hopkins write both extended and contracted forms of the normal sonnet made him also ceaselessly and restlessly experiment on the very constitution of the English language; and though this has given us some of his finest triumphs, it has also beguiled him occasionally to prosodical and linguistic shallows and miseries. He begins on several occasions a new line with the latter part of a broken word—

> To what serves mortal beauty—dangerous; does set danc-
> *ing* blood—the O-seal-that-so feature . . .[19]

> . . . . . I wear-
> y of idle a being but by where wars are rife.[20]

Compound words are sometimes broken in the most artificial and violent manner as in 'wind-lilylocks-laced'. At other times compound words are concocted in so arbitrary a fashion that they produce mere jingles—

> Tatter-tassel-tangled and dingle-a-dangled
> Dandy-hung dainty head . . .[21]

Similarly, Hopkins's rhymes are occasionally altogether far-fetched or even monstrous. In 'The Loss of the

[19] *Poems*, No. 38. [20] ibid., No. 44.
[21] ibid., No. 64.

Eurydice', Hopkins rhymes 'eternal' with 'burn all' in the last stanza; objection to this particular rhyme, however, is dismissed by Mr Megroz as coming from 'the carping Satan of routine-cultured response'.[22] It may be that when the poem is chanted at a stretch, the current of one's emotional response may prevent one from noticing the vulgarity of rhyming 'eternal' with 'burn all'; but a defect it remains none the less. In the same poem there are other untenable rhymes like 'fully on, bullion', 'England, mingle? and', 'coast or, snowstorm', 'suit; he, beauty', 'busy to, visited'; elsewhere we have the no less impossible 'a boon he on, Communion', 'ride and jar, did: disregarded', 'justices, eye he is', and 'I am, and: diamond'. Bridges must have pointed out many of these aberrations during Hopkins's lifetime; and Hopkins's reply was: 'Some of my rhymes I regret, but they are past changing, grubs in amber: there are only a few of these; others are unassailable; some others again there are which *malignity may munch* at but the Muses love.'[23]

Hopkins's poetry, then, has its defects; defects in imagery and defects in style, the former wrecking the understanding on the rock of far-fetched conceits and the latter offending the ear by doing violence to grammar or to the genius of the language. Generally speaking, Hopkins kept his theories in their place and exploited the potentialities of the language successfully and occasionally even triumphantly; but, now and then, his theories got the better of him, and proved the Djin in the Arabian Nights: and then he became a martyr to his own theories. The Jesuit and the man, the poet and the man of action, the writer of lucid and flowing prose and the poet wrestling with words to

[22] *Modern English Poetry*, p. 243.
[23] *Letters*, I, p. 180.

express himself—these were inescapable dichotomies battling within Hopkins. And the significant fact about him was, as Mr Michael Roberts remarks, 'not that he invented a style different from the current poetic style, but that, working in subterranean fashion, he moulded a style which expressed the tension and disorder that he found inside himself'.[24] He strained every nerve, exerted all his faculties, to escape this tension and this disorder and to establish 'a coincidence of grammatical, emotional metrical stress'[25] that shall hymn the harmony he was seeking; but success in this unusual adventure, though it did come to him in poems like 'The Windhover' and in some of the later sonnets, could not be uniform; nor was such success to be expected every time. But Hopkins had always enough self-criticism to see his own major defects and to define clearly in which direction progress for him was possible. In a letter to Bridges, written in 1879, Hopkins confesses: 'No doubt my poetry errs on the side of oddness. I hope in time to have a more balanced and Miltonic style . . . it is the virtue of design, pattern, or inscape to be distinctive and it is the vice of distinctiveness to become queer. This vice I cannot have escaped.'[26] But the seeming oddity is merely the outer shell, almost forbidding one to taste the kernel within; but with sympathetic and informed study 'the grammatical uncertainties and metrical oddities will divide and rinse clear. And what before seemed "masses of impracticable quartz" may now become a jewel-case marvellously wrought and lovely to behold, a monstrance, as it were, for a Living Flame.'[27] And then Hopkins will come to his own; and he will find his place high up in the scroll of English poets.

[24] *The Faber Book of Modern Verse*, Introduction, p. 4.
[25] Welby, *A Popular History of English Poetry* (1933), pp. 282-3.
[26] *Letters*, I, p. 66.   [27] Lahey, p. 106.

XVIII. CONCLUSION

THE influence of Hopkins on contemporary poets is admittedly considerable. Eliot and Auden, Spender and Cecil Day Lewis, and the later Yeats have all, in one way or another, been responsive to Hopkins's poetical achievements. The following lines from Mr W. H. Auden very clearly reveal the influence of Hopkins—

> O watcher in the dark, you wake
> Our dream of waking, we feel
> Your finger on the flesh that has been skinned.
> By your bright day
> See clear what we were doing, that we were vile.

It is impossible when reading these lines not to be reminded of Hopkins's famous sonnet beginning with 'I wake and feel the fell of dark, not day'. Elsewhere, Mr Auden uncannily reproduces the characteristic rhythm and interior rhymes of Hopkins's poetry—

> Me, March, you do with your movements master
>   and rock
> With wing-whirl, whale-wallow, silent budding
>   of cell . . .
> Here at the small field's ending pause
>
> Where the chalk wall falls to the foam, and its
>   tall ledges
> Oppose the pluck
> And knock of the tide,
> And the shingle scrambles after the sucking surf,
>   and the gull lodges
> A moment on its sheer side . . .
>
> Which of you waking early and watching daybreak
> Will not hasten in heart, handsome, aware of wonder
> At light unleashed, advancing, a leader of movement,
> Breaking life surf or turf on road and roof . . .

CONCLUSION

Passages and word-combinations like 'sea-dingle', 'rock-face', 'whorled unsubtle ears', and scores of others constitute Mr Auden's homage to Hopkins's technical mastery.

Eliot's debt to Hopkins, though perhaps less open, is no less vital. There is the same allusiveness and compression in Eliot as there is in Hopkins, and the same preoccupation with themes inspired by Christianity; their rhythms are equally, if not to an equal degree, flexible; and, again, their assonances and internal rhymes are equally suggestive. A poem like Eliot's 'Burnt Norton' inevitably invites comparison with Hopkins's 'That Nature is a Heraclitean Fire and of the comfort of the Resurrection'; and often they both succeed in charging the seeming commonplaces of conversational speech with the fervour and intensity of genuine poetry.

Several other poets of today betray Hopkins's influence. It is clear, for instance, in these lines from Mr Cecil Day Lewis's 'The Magnetic Mountain'—

> Now to be with you, elate, unshared,
> My kestrel joy, O hoverer in wind,
> Over the query furiously at rest
> Chaired on shoulders of shouting wind . . .

The reference to 'The Windhover' is unmistakable. Further, the following passages from W. B. Yeats's later writings show how even he was influenced by the work of Hopkins—

> Turning and turning in the widening gyre
> The falcon cannot hear the falconer;
> Things fall apart; the centre cannot hold . . .
>
> I declare this tower is my symbol; I declare
> This winding, gyring, treadmill of a stair is my
>   ancestral stair . . .

However, the poets of today (excepting, perhaps, Mr Eliot) are unwilling to take adequate pains in translating nebulous ideas and impressions into living poetic images, and hence rarely are they able to give us poems in which, as in Hopkins's best, alliteration and assonance, the appositeness of phrase and the impulsion of sound combine to become a potent spell, an irresistible continuum of incantation. Moreover, as Miss Deutsch remarks, 'What Hopkins has in common with the metaphysical school, the probing of his own mind, the wrestling of the intellectual with the sensual imagination—these younger poets do not evince so clearly.'[1] Finally, modernists like Auden, Spender and Cecil Day Lewis have little or no faith in religion, excepting in Communism itself as a religion; and in consequence their poetry lacks the core of purposive and creative faith that sustains Hopkins's poetry, though he too was 'in a manner' a Communist, but a Communist with a difference, such a vast deal of difference.

Hopkins was a poet, and to us he is primarily a poet; and as a poet his influence is growing.[2] But it is well to remember here that Hopkins was a penetrating critic as well. The minute attention he gave to the poems of Bridges, Dixon and Patmore helped them to improve and amend their work before publication. Whether in the statement of general principles of criticism or in the criticism of particular authors or works, Hopkins is equally discriminating, illuminating, and, almost as a rule, convincing. Many of his judgements have stood the test of time. Hopkins did not like Keats's vehement emphasis on

[1] *This Modern Poetry*, p. 198.
[2] cf. Herbert Read: '. . . no poet of recent times is likely to exercise such a potent influence as Hopkins. . . . Hopkins understood the technique of English poetry as no poet since Dryden understood it.' (*A Coat of Many Colours*, p. 160.)

a life of sensations; but he had divination enough to write: 'Keats' genius was so astonishing, unequalled at his age and scarcely surpassed at any, that one may surmise whether if he had lived he would not have rivalled Shakespeare.'[3] This is exactly what the late Sir Sidney Colvin and Mr John Middleton Murry have been trying to make out in their monumental studies. Hopkins, again, has penetration enough to defend Browning's *Ring and the Book* from the attacks of Canon Dixon: 'I was greatly struck with the skill in which he displayed the facts from different points of view: this is masterly, and to do it through three volumes more shews a great body of genius.'[4] His remarks on Carlyle are interesting: 'I do not like his pampered and affected style, I hate his principles, I burn most that he worships and worship most that he burns, I cannot respect (no one now can) his character, but the force of his genius seems to me gigantic. He seems to me to have more humour than any writer of ours except Shakespeare. I should have called him the greatest genius of Scotland.'[5] Elsewhere Hopkins describes Carlyle's writings as 'most inefficacious-strenuous heaven-protestations, caterwaul, and Cassandra-wailings'[6]—truly an admirable imitation of Carlylese as well as an accurate labelling of his copious output. Criticism of one's own contemporaries is always a difficult thing; one cannot cultivate the detachment that is the first requisite of the sober judge; and yet these judgements of Hopkins's have worn well. There are exaggerations, too, now and then: 'I think Robert Lewis Stevenson shows more genius in a page than Scott in a volume.'[7] Elsewhere he places Stevenson above Thomas Hardy;[8] but

[3] *Letters*, II, p. 6.
[5] ibid., p. 59.
[7] ibid., p. 228.
[4] ibid., p. 74.
[6] *Letters*, I, p. 27.
[8] ibid., p. 239.

it is significant that even so early as 1887, Hopkins was able to look upon Hardy as a man of 'pure and direct genius'.⁹ About Swinburne, Hopkins always writes intelligently; and these remarks clinchingly assess the later works of Swinburne with an almost disarming finality: 'It is all now a "self-drawing web"; a perpetual functioning of genius without truth, feeling, or any adequate matter to be at function on.'¹⁰

An earnest student of Greek, Hopkins's views on Greek drama and the Greek tragedians are profoundly suggestive. 'What a noble genius Aeschylus had!' he writes to Bridges: 'Besides the swell and pomp of words for which he is famous there is in him a touching consideration and manly tenderness; also an earnestness of spirit and would-be piety by which the man makes himself felt through the playwright. This is not so with Sophocles, who is only the learned and sympathetic dramatist; and much less Euripides.'¹¹ Such criticism must sharpen the edge of our awareness to the multiverses of Greek tragedy. Talking of the 'Unities', Hopkins takes 'unity of action' to mean 'not simplicity of plot' but 'connectedness of plot';¹² in this matter, again, Hopkins shows his great insight and creative understanding. But by far Hopkins's most solid achievement in creative and constructive criticism is his Platonic dialogue on the origin of beauty, to which reference has already been made in an earlier chapter. It was probably written when Hopkins was at Oxford, and, probably again, it was written for perusal and correction by Walter Pater. The essays on 'Poetic Diction', 'Rhythm in Poetry', and 'Poetry and Verse' are some of his other more ambitious undertakings in criticism.

⁹ *Letters*, I, p. 251. ¹⁰ ibid., p. 304.
¹¹ ibid., p. 256. ¹² *Letters*, II, p. 113.

Hopkins the critic was an acute intelligence; his judgements were based on knowledge and commonsense; he no doubt held strong opinions on a number of points, but he did not allow these to warp his judgements on other people's literary works; and, above all, he had the capacity not merely to assess the worth of the particulars but also to grasp and estimate the significance of the background. Hopkins the poet was a daring innovator—but indubitably a poet still. But the man was greater than both the poet and the critic; the more we know him from his letters, the more we regret that his achievements as a poet and as a critic are not at all commensurate with his great attainments. His being a Jesuit perhaps initially hampered his literary activities; the urge to express himself through poetry and the determination not to allow such activities to interfere with the vocation he had chosen were throughout pitted one against the other, and gleams of this struggle can be noticed in his correspondence no less than in his poetry. Ultimately he found the idiom that will correctly indicate this tension within himself—a tension that we have no doubt he resolved in the end and sublimated into a devouring love of Christ.[13] His brother Jesuits have feelingly testified to his singular goodness and God-intoxicatedness; having early chosen a religious life, he lived it through sincerely, unobtrusively, almost happily. It became more and more difficult to dissociate the man, the uniquely human friend and blood-relation, from the ardent Jesuit, dedicating his energies and faculties to the greater glory of God; but till the end Gerard Hopkins preserved his individuality almost miraculously without in any

---

[13] cf. Pick, p. 129: '. . . his poetry is the story of the relationship of his soul to God . . . his poems are really love poems . . .'

manner failing as Father Hopkins, S.J. His letters to his friends, to Bridges especially, are the letters that a very friendly angel might write to one yet inhabiting the earth. But even Hopkins, so wise and so tolerant and so full of the milk of human kindness, now and then lost his balance —especially when politics were under discussion. Yet these rare verbal excesses on Gladstone and Parnell and the rest reveal the too human political animal that Hopkins was in unguarded moments, and endear him to us in spite of his opinions. Such lapses are the proverbial exceptions that prove the rule that Hopkins was ever gentle, ever considerate to his 'enemies', ever eager and able to see the other man's point of view. His humility was amazing; again and again he called himself a 'blackguard', and gravely warned Bridges: 'The quality of a gentleman is so very fine a thing that it seems to me one should not be at all hasty in concluding that one possesses it.'[14] Though he has a fine sense of humour, it but insinuates its fun into our hearts; it does not explode, it does not wound; and he has no cynicism in his composition. On the contrary he believed in taking things seriously, in life as well as in literature. He maintained that 'a kind of touchstone of the highest or most living art is seriousness; not gravity but the being in earnest with your subject—reality.'[15] He could not be flippant, nor light-headed, nor half-hearted in anything he undertook to do—a letter, a notice, a lecture, or even the assessing of answer-books; he must always give his best. Such concentration and such dogged perseverence with his duties, whether or not they were congenial, gradually undermined his strength and exhausted his reserves of vitality; he knew he could not go on in that stride, but still he went his usual way, breathless, panting;

---

[14] *Letters*, I, p. 175. [15] ibid., p. 225.

the inevitable happened; Gerard Hopkins aged quickly, aged before his prime, fell ill, and so died. He died at peace with himself and with his parents, and with his God as well; and he died thinking presumably that his poems, so many of them, in which he had written himself out, would remain for a time in manuscript, and then be forgotten altogether. But Bridges preserved them, and has now given them and their once obscure author a new lease of life and made him one of the immortals of English literature.

We have traversed a wide field. What shall we say in conclusion regarding the puzzling phenomenon of Gerard Manley Hopkins? Let us admit that Hopkins was odd, most odd, he was certainly original, disconcertingly original. Once he wrote: 'The effect of studying masterpieces is to make me admire and do otherwise. So it must be on every original artist to some degree, on me to a marked degree.'[16] Hopkins, then, dared to explore new regions, and, may be, he stumbled sometimes, but more often than not he did courageously stand his ground and annex new and valuable territory to the realm of English poetry. Is not Gerard Hopkins entitled to a large measure of gratitude from lovers of English poetry? No doubt, in the ethereal regions of the spirit, Father Hopkins has his God-anointed high seat, and is an example to fellow Catholics and fellow Jesuits all the world over. But consider him simply as a poet, an artist whose interests ranged from architecture to music, and still he is most formidable; watch him as he sits, with quiet dignity, on Parnassus, delicately executing another rich jewelled phrase that shall flash forth the 'instress' of the divided world and 'inscape' its underlying Order—and you feel convinced that this Jack, joke, poet, Jesuit priest, immortal diamond, is immortal diamond.

[16] *Letters*, I, p. 291.

SELECT BIBLIOGRAPHY

Words in brackets at the end of the first seven entries in this bibliography denote the short titles by which the books are mentioned in the footnotes.

Poems of Gerard Manley Hopkins, edited with notes by Robert Bridges. Second edition by Charles Williams. Oxford University Press, 1930. (*Poems*.)

The Letters of Gerard Manley Hopkins to Robert Bridges, edited by Claude Colleer Abbott. Oxford University Press, 1935. (*Letters, I.*)

The Correspondence of Gerard Manley Hopkins and Richard Watson Dixon, edited by C. C. Abbott. Oxford University Press, 1935. (*Letters, II.*)

Further Letters of Gerard Manley Hopkins, including his correspondence with Coventry Patmore; edited by C. C. Abbott. Oxford University Press, 1938. (*Letters, III.*)

The Note-Books and Papers of Gerard Manley Hopkins, edited by Humphry House. Oxford University Press, 1937. (*Note-Books*.)

Gerard Manley Hopkins, by G. F. Lahey, S.J. Oxford University Press, 1930. (*Lahey*.)

Gerard Manley Hopkins—Priest and Poet, by John Pick. Oxford University Press, 1942. (*Pick*.)

Four Independents, by Daniel Sargent. Sheed & Ward, 1935.

A Philosophy of Form, by E. I. Watkin. Sheed & Ward, 1935.

The Spirit of Mediaeval Philosophy, by Etienne Gilson. Sheed & Ward, 1936.

The Philosophy of St. Bonaventure, by Etienne Gilson. Sheed & Ward, 1938.

The Poetry of Gerard Manley Hopkins, A Survey and a Commentary, by Elsie Elizabeth Phare. Cambridge University Press, 1933.

Modern English Poetry, by R. L. Megroz. Ivor Nicholson & Watson, 1933.

Essays & Studies by Members of the English Association, Vol. V. Clarendon Press, 1914.

Selected Poems of Coventry Patmore, edited by Derek Patmore. Phoenix Library. Chatto & Windus.

English Critical Essays, Twentieth Century. World's Classics. Oxford University Press.

New Bearings on English Poetry, by F. R. Leavis. Chatto & Windus, 1932.

The Poems of John Donne, edited by Sir H. J. C. Grierson. Oxford University Press, 1933.